365 Days
of Grief
and Love

VICKIE MONROE GUERRY

Charleston, SC
www.PalmettoPublishing.com

365 Days of Grief and Love

Copyright © 2021 by Vickie Monroe Guerry

First Edition

Paperback ISBN: 978-1-63837-610-1

Prologue

No one may ever read these words. That's ok.

I am writing out of a sense of near desperation to convey some thoughts, feelings, emotions and anger that I have experienced since the death of my husband. Hopefully, the writing will help in some way. If indeed, these words help another person walking the grief trail, all the better.

Although the grief of losing my husband began prior to October 17, 2019, I begin there.

Thursday, October 17, 2019

It's 3:00 a.m. and I am sitting in a chair, watching my husband. He awakens, drinks a sip of water, then falls back to sleep. The morphine is still working. I go up to bed to try and get a little sleep in order to face the next day.

It's 5:30. I wake up, go down to check on him and he is gone. Alone, he died alone. I cover him with the sheet he has crumbled under his legs, kiss him and go upstairs. I take a shower. I need this time by myself, with the knowledge that I have, to process, to take deep breaths, to prepare for the day. Somehow, I feel that Tom and I are sharing something, some knowledge, some wisdom, that no one else can share. Our son has stayed the past two nights with us and shared the vigil of waiting. I go into his old room, wake him up and give him the news.

It's 6:30. I call Tom's daughter, a teacher, before she can leave for school. Then I call Hospice per instructed. Then I text our sisters, his brother, our minister friend, our lawyer friend, and a few others that needed to know quickly. This will continue most of the day, when I have a second to go to the call list that we had prepared days before.

Hospice was amazing. The nurse came quickly, was kind, caring and competent. She called the necessary personnel, cleaned Tom's body, talked with me.

Our two dogs, Barkley and Rascal, seemed to understand. They both stayed beside Tom's hospital bed as a protective force. They were quiet and watchful. Somehow, they knew.

Woody showed up and later brought Chick-fil-A food (I don't remember what). Mac came. Donna and Carl came. Amy and John came.

A neighbor friend brought toilet paper, paper towels and a notebook that she had put together to record food, flowers, addresses, information, etc. We used it.

The day is a blur. My phone never stopped ringing, nor did the doorbell. Lots of care, lots of support, loads of love. It's what we do as a people.

Amy and John (Tom's daughter and son-in-law) left at about 1:00, and Ben and I headed to the funeral home. You are in such shock and decisions have to be made. Checks have to be written. We had done a lot of planning, had written an obituary, planned the service, so it was quicker than it would have been.

About 5:30, Ben and I decided to grab some dinner in a quiet restaurant to escape from the house. That was a good plan. Even as we were attempting to leave, people were coming to the house. No complaints about the goodness of the people in our lives, just a realization that we were in a type of shock, totally overwhelmed,

Thus, endeth the day.

Friday, October 18

A new day dawns. Doorbell ringing, phone ringing, decisions to be made.

A sense of everything being surreal surrounds me. I go through the motions, answer questions, try and eat.

Working on service with Ben and Amy.

Looking at a bare sunroom except for the piano. The location where Tom's hospital bed was, is now an empty space. Nothing is normal.

Ben and I had a meeting with the two ministers at our home to discuss the service. Tom had carefully picked out the hymns that he wanted, the scripture that he wanted, and had declared that he wanted no eulogy, but for Ben to speak and Caison to play the piano for one hymn. He had asked Caison, his oldest grandson and a music major in college, to play "Come Thou Fount of Every Blessing." He jokingly told Caison he had to pick the song so Caison wouldn't play hip-hop! All of these decisions helped us in the planning, and so all we really needed to determine was the format. It still was more difficult than I imagined. Ben stated emphatically that he could not speak following music, so that request was honored. Amy and her family offered to sing the hymn as Caison played. A beautiful wooden music stand that Tom had made Ben as a Christmas present one year when he was in the high school band was taken to be used for the interpreters for the deaf.

We contacted interpreters, musicians, florist. I almost forgot the flowers, but I wanted two small arrangements on either side of the pulpit. Asked for purple and orange, Clemson colors.

Saturday, October 19

I remember talking with out-of-town friends about hotels, etc., and inviting folks here for lunch after the service, which the neighborhood was preparing, and dinner the night before, which my former workplace was preparing. The church brought food nonstop.

Since Tom had elected to be cremated, there was a waiting period of several days in order to get the death certificate and then arrange the cremation. We had selected an urn the day before while at the funeral home.

Sunday, October 20

Sundays were always special in our family. Having a minister in the family, we were in church on Sundays. However, since Tom was a professor of religion, he supplied for churches around the Lowcountry and did the occasional interim. One of his favorite stories was when Ben was about three and Tom was preaching in a small country church. They had an intercom in the nursery so the workers could hear the service. One of the gentlemen working in the nursery that day told Tom that Ben was playing on the floor with some cars, and when Tom stood up to begin his sermon, Ben looked up and said, "Oh, that's just my dad, trying to preach." And preach he did and could. I told him in a letter one time that his words spoke to me from the very beginning, and taught me and made me think.

The past eight years, after retirement from the university faculty, he had taken a position with the French Huguenot Church as Associate Pastor. A Huguenot himself, and this church the church that we were married in, it was a natural fit. Those years were very good years.

And now it is Sunday. No Tom. No church.

Monday, October 21

I have little recall of these days, as life just kept moving around me.

I do remember making a detailed list of family and friends of the family to sit in the small pews at the church. I worked hard on this, placing family members according to their relationship to Tom and then to me. Our church has small pews with doors, and four persons is the max possible, if you have small people. I made two copies, one for me and one for the funeral home director.

That ended up being a waste of time.

So true to nature, no one really listened. People fell in line and walked to the church, however…no one really cared.

I think as much as anything, it was something to do, to keep me from falling apart, to plan, to organize.

Tuesday, October 22

Linda arrived from Seattle.

Linda and I had become friends the summer before our junior year in high school when her family moved to Morganton and joined our church. We roomed together our freshman year in college and remained in contact through the years. We both divorced and remarried, had children. She lived in Canada for years, but the communication lines were intact.

She flew in to Charleston and stayed with me until Thursday. What a gift. Ben and I picked her up at the airport, and the three of us went to Poe's Tavern on Sullivan's Island for lunch. I am not sure after we got home that any of us sat down again for hours.

Friends and family from out of town began arriving. My former school where I'd served as a speech pathologist for many years and retired from in 2013 provided dinner that night for probably forty people. It was good to have people close to us there as it was a diversion and a support for both Ben and me. I think especially the presence of my great-nieces and -nephews was so positive as children bring such joy. Woody and Kristen joined us for dinner, which was a comfort.

Ben had two friends come in from out of state who stayed with him, and he needed to be at his own apartment and have some space from me and from this house. He could do that without guilt as Linda was with me.

We headed to bed very early as she had literally flown a redeye from Seattle and had gotten little to no sleep.

Thank goodness for paper plates and napkins.

Wednesday, October 23

I wake up early and Linda is still asleep in the guest room. I take this time and silence to try and pull myself together and to ask for strength to get through the day.

We drink our coffee, get dressed and Ben picks us up about 9:30 to head to the church. Grant and Kate, two of Ben's friends, are with us, and we head downtown Charleston. Woody has graciously given us his parking spot, as it is mid-week Charleston.

As we are walking up to 44 Queen where we are meeting with family, close friends and clergy prior to the service, we see the two interpreters—Dean and Shari. Introductions are made and they come inside. I had asked them to join us for this part so that my deaf sister and brother-in-law had communication, which I could not handle at this point in time.

We all crowded into the church parlor, and I attempted introductions, which was hard. I also read the seating arrangements, which was a waste of breath. Oh well, minor details.

As we followed the funeral home person down the street to the church, several of our church elders were outside passing out programs. I also remember a horse and buggy had stopped to let us walk. Tourists were standing silently on the street corners, and all was quiet as we passed. That seemed surreal also, like we were acting a role. When we got to the narthex, I realized that the church was packed.

We got through it. Ben did an amazing job speaking. Amy, John and their sons sang beautifully, even though Keller became very upset during the hymn. The music was lovely, and I think Tom would have been pleased with the service. The programs were perfect. My brother-in-law, Carl, led the brief graveside committal of the ashes. Carl had conducted our wedding in 1986 at The French Huguenot Church, so he took us from the beginning to the end.

The reception that the church provided was beyond anything I could have asked for. Delicious food (I heard), and plenty of it. Tom loved his Bloody Mary after church on Sundays, and they had a Bloody Mary bar in his honor. Someone put a glass of Pinot Grigio in my hand, and another lady took that and gave me a Diet Dr. Pepper, which was what I wanted. Tom also loved Moon Pies and they had a huge bowl of Moon Pies. Lots and lots of people, hugs, tears. It was overwhelming the outpouring of love for Tom and for our family.

We finally broke free when most folks had gone and headed home. Linda had gone with Elise and Sylvia to get things ready at the house for the luncheon, so it was just the four of us. Mary had stayed at the house during the service to prepare but also to have someone in the house. Our neighborhood came together to provide this luncheon, along with leftover food from the night before and food Camille brought from the church as well.

Lots of family and out-of-town friends came by. Lots of food. A couple of Ben's local friends who had to work came on their lunch hour and ate with us.

One of my few smiles that day occurred when my great-niece, Winnie, who was eighteen months old, came walking across the floor with a Moon Pie clutched in her hand. I thought, "Does Jenny know?" and then I thought, "It's OK today." Still makes me smile. It would have made Tom smile too.

Another was when Finn, another great-niece, sat in the garage waiting for Linda and me to return after taking recycling down to Elise's recycling bin. We had no idea the child was still in the garage.

Ben opened the door and there she sat, clutching a stuffed dog I had given her and waiting. The little things that we remember.

Rascal, Ben's dog, found an empty dining room with a table full of food and hurriedly swallowed some cold cuts whole. Upon discovery, and Linda taking him outside, he proceeded to throw them all up.

After several hours, everyone was gone. Grant had to drive back to Atlanta to work the next day. Kate was spending the night and leaving for Raleigh in the a.m., so she and Ben went to dinner to have some time to catch up. Linda and I were alone, with Barkley.

We fixed bowls of hot chili that my neighbor had prepared, some homemade cornbread, and a glass of wine and went out to the screened-in porch and settled in. It was good that Linda was there. We talked about the day, cried, laughed and ate.

These are my memories of that day.

Ben has reminded me and made me laugh several times about how Grant was dressed in all black and looked like an undertaker. Ben had asked Grant to be up on the platform with him in case Ben could not get through his comments. Grant graciously agreed.

Thursday, October 24, 2019

Spent a busy morning with Linda, Francie and Ben trying to freeze food, give away food, and downsize the amounts in the refrigerator.

Took Linda to the airport to fly back to Seattle.

Realization that this will be my first night alone.

As I write and try and reconstruct these days months later, I notice the lack of emotion conveyed in these pages. But actually, I think that is true in that you are too exhausted, both physically and mentally, to show emotions. You move through the days like a robot, on automatic. The emotions and grief will come later.

Friday, October 25, 2019

I went to work at Meeting Street Academy this a.m. They were surprised to see me, and perhaps it was too early. I had been out of work for two weeks and the kids had missed speech therapy. As I told the principal, Dirk, "This is my happy place." I needed the kids, and the distraction. I only work two half days per week, so thought I might as well get Monday over with, and it got me out of an empty house.

Saturday, October 26, 2019

Today is Donna's birthday. She and Carl took me to lunch, on her birthday.

Ben headed to Clemson for the game. He already had tickets and I encouraged him to go.

I watched the Tigers and the Tarheels games alone.

Sunday, October 27, 2019

Another Sunday and no church. Not ready to face that yet.

Began to get organized with thank-you notes for food.

Throughout the past few months, my neighbor Francie and I began to walk every morning that I did not work. It was a lifesaver for me, to get out, to chat, to exercise. Even when things were at their worst, we continued our walks. Tom encouraged them, as he knew how much I needed them. I would get him set up with the newspaper and coffee and sometimes breakfast before we walked. After he died, we continued our walks, before sunup. We walked with flashlights to watch for snakes because it was easier not to run into people. She will never know what this time meant to me. Her grace, her laughter, her listening ears.

Monday, October 28, 2019

Went to work again. So glad that I went in on Friday to get those caring comments behind me.

Had an appointment with the bank to get Ben's name on all accounts and checks. Had to provide death certificate. Is this becoming real?

Plenty of food, so Ben and I put meals together from the refrigerator.

Tuesday, October 29, 2019

So, my 2007 Volvo is twelve years old and not roadworthy, especially if I am traveling alone. Ben and I go to look at cars, only to look, but I end up driving a 2017 home! Quite an upgrade for me. Traded in the old Volvo. Ben cleaned up and posted Tom's 2008 Jetta and sold it on Craigslist in four hours!! Wish everything had been as easy as the X3 purchase.

Wednesday, October 30, 2019

Worked this a.m. Fun to do Halloween activities with three- and four-year-old kids. So good for me.

Called State Farm on the way to the mountains! Ben and I decided to take one night and head to Asheville to hopefully see some late color and to breathe mountain air. Once a mountain girl, always a mountain girl, and the mountains have always been my place—for comfort, relaxation, renewal. I needed this.

Thursday, October 31, 2019

Woke up to crisp mountain air and a pumpkin spice latte!

Stopped at an apple orchard on the way back to Charleston.

A girlfriend came over for dinner, to chat and to have a glass of wine. Ben spent time with friends.

Halloween night was always fun at our house. Tom took Ben trick or treating when he was little, and he always went out when he was older. We allowed him to decorate the yard however he wanted, and we had graveyards and spider webs and all manner of decorations. I manned the door for the trick or treaters, and Tom's sister, June, came over. Chili was always on our menu and lots of laughter. Tom played spooky music on the piano when I opened the door. None of that this year. June now lives in Florida and is too ill to travel and the piano player is gone. His silent piano is a reminder.

Friday, November 1, 2019

Ours was not the typical boy-meets-girl love story, but it was our love story. My husband was my parents' minister, then my minister, then a friend, all before he became a lover. We connected through a common passion for working with the deaf—and humor. We both were married to other people, and after divorces and finding ourselves in a new state and city, we began to date. Again, the common initial thread was deafness as both of us were involved in organizations that worked with deaf people.

Learning to trust again after broken marriages took time, and we dated several years before we married. He was forty-seven, I was thirty-five. We immediately began to try to get pregnant and after six months were referred to a fertility specialist. Tom had two daughters from his previous marriage and I had no children. We also began the process of adopting, thinking that we could give a good home to a deaf child. But we became pregnant, and when I was thirty-eight and he was fifty, God gave us a son. What a glorious day! Every day of his life has been a gift, and one that we never took lightly. He was the apple of his dad's eye and his older dad exposed him to activities that another dad might not have...gardening, camping, reading, woodworking, building decks and barns. They traveled each summer for years to a father/son Cubs game and varied the locations as well as the teams that the Cubs were playing.

We also traveled as a family to various sites around the country with my job and then a memorable three-week trip to England and Scotland, with one week in France, Germany, Switzerland and the

Netherlands. We found the small village in France from where the first Guerry had come to Charleston in the 1600s and found Guerrys on the tombstones.

Our marriage was not perfect, but then neither were we. I regret the times we wasted fighting and not loving, pouting and not talking, crying and not holding each other. But our love never wavered through everything. We supported each other professionally and personally. We enjoyed lots of the same things together but had our individual likes too, such as my love for UNC basketball and his disdain for basketball in general!

But this writing is not about our life together but about my grief and this process. Well, maybe it is about our life, because without our love, there would not be grief.

Saturday November 2, 2019

Spent some time cleaning this house. Watched the Tigers and the Heels, but had Ben this time.

These games were always fun in our house. Tom being a Clemson man and me a UNC girl, we laughed and picked and supported each other's team. Ben being a Clemson grad and the Tigers on a big win streak didn't hurt the excitement either.

We have pictures of Ben's first trip to Chapel Hill and his first trip to Clemson. These memories are good and they are difficult. So grateful to have them, but the pain is worse because of them too.

Sunday, November 3, 2019

So, took a breath and made it to church. Ben went with me. Rough morning as I cried from the time I walked into the narthex. People were amazing and caring. Woody mentioned Tom in his sermon. Sitting in that pew and no Tom on the platform was so hard. Not hearing his voice doing the benediction was strange, and uncomfortable. We were married here in 1986, we buried him in the church cemetery in 2019. A sacred place, but a difficult place. Maybe it was too soon.

Wanted to support Woody as it was his first sermon at our church. It was right to be there, and it was all wrong.

Monday, November 4, 2019

A friend and coworker told me about a man who helps young men prepare for job interviews. I was able to get Tom's suits, dress shirts, some of his ties, dress shoes and donate them to this man. Of course, Tom wore a size fourteen shoe! Hopefully, at least one of these young men will have a big foot.

Tom would have approved of this.

I frequently find myself thinking, "What would Tom do? What would Tom say?" Having been partners for many years, through rough and through happy times, decisions were made together. So now I say, "What do I do?"

Words to an old song say, "Hold your head up high, and you'll never walk alone." But I do.

Tuesday, November 5, 2019

Grief is a funny thing, an individual thing, a surreal thing. We go along with daily routines, and then BAM, some minor word or song or action knocks you flat. One feels that after weeks of grief, when people say, "How are you?" that they actually want an "Oh, I'm fine." But that isn't true and perhaps will never be true. We go through our routine actions and move on with life and the "new normal" as people like to say, but each step is agony.

It's amazing too how much we learn. During the dying process that I experienced, it was progressive and slow. We had time to talk and to plan. So many things (legal and medical) that we thought were all taken care of, but we found out that we needed to do more. You can't plan for those things. Like a DHEC DNR...we had a legal DNR, but we needed a DHEC DNR. Caregivers like my son and myself learned about oxygen and the caring for the equipment, about how we would approach hurricane season with days without electricity to refuel the oxygen tanks, about morphine and how to administer it, how to change sheets on a bed with your loved one still in it. A constant learning curve while shuffling through daily chores and personal needs.

How do people do this without a village? We were so very blessed to have family, friends and neighbors, as well as church family who were here and constant in their support and care. What would we have done without them?

It is hectic, it is exhausting, it is surreal. Then there is the service to plan and the stone to select and the thank-you notes to write and then that too is gone.

And you are alone. Again, I was blessed with a son who lived two miles away, who came daily to eat with me, to have "happy hour" with me, to talk and to listen. I had a sister and brother-in-law who lived nearby and who brought food, and more importantly, they brought love. But I was still alone those other hours of the day and night.

Wednesday, November 6, 2019

I have found, going through drawers, an amazing number of glasses. Some are prescription, some are reading glasses. Maybe twenty to thirty pairs. I have learned that our ophthalmologist's office accepts these glasses and sends them overseas to countries where people don't have access to eyecare. Heading there today to donate.

Tom also wore hearing aids, so I emailed his audiologist and found out about a hearing aid bank. I need to call them.

We have so much and there are multiple people who do without necessary items daily. Trying to do something helpful with Tom's possessions because I believe he would want that. Twenty-six years of living in this same house and thirty-three years of marriage, we did accumulate.

Thursday, November 7, 2019

Tonight, was the annual oyster roast at the church courtyard. Ben and I decided to go. He had never been and Tom and I always went. It was hard, but also good. Good to be outside, to be with loving people, to eat some Lowcountry oysters. At least it provided some variety from this sameness.

Friday, November 8, 2019

Worked this a.m. to make up one of the days of therapy for the kids that I had missed.

Met Stuart and Susan for lunch.

I am noticing as I go through my calendar to try and reconstruct these days, that the common thread of friends and family show up a lot. People truly don't understand what the little things mean during this journey.

I remember going into a funeral home for a visitation one time with my husband, and I said that I didn't know what to say to this person who had lost someone. Tom said, "People don't remember what you said, they remember that you were there." And oh, do we...Some friends have tried to be there but just don't know how. They want me to be fine, to be whole again and to move on. They don't have the compassion to just listen, to let me cry or vent or scream. They feel that there has been enough time now. But how does one measure time and grief?

Saturday, November 9, 2019

Tom was diagnosed with a chronic lung infection (MAC) twelve years ago. We were told then that it was treatable, but not curable. For the next ten and a half years, he functioned normally with an occasional flare-up. Then in June 2018, we took our last vacation. We flew into Boston and drove through Massachusetts and Maine. We visited the homes and graves of famous authors including Thoreau, Alcott, Emerson, Hawthorne and went to the Eric Carle Museum. Both of us were thrilled about this trip. Tom did all the planning. I did all the driving—which was a first on these trips. We stayed on the coast of Maine one night and ate lobster. We stayed in Boston the last night and attended a Red Sox game at Fenway. It was a really memorable trip. However, on the trip home, Tom began feeling bad and never really recovered fully. Thus, began eighteen months of decline. He continued to serve the church, to preach, to do weddings, and to do his writings. Most other activities slowed, as he no longer had the energy for his woodworking or much else. We occasionally went to dinner with friends, but mainly we were at home together.

In July, 2018 we traveled to Morganton, NC, for the funeral of a friend's father. Linda, Karen and Tommy's father had died at age ninety-seven. He had lived a full, long life and left behind a grieving family and a heartbroken wife, Louise. This would be the last trip to Morganton for Wendell (I can name switch). My hometown, the place where we first met, where my parents are buried, where he served as a much-loved pastor. At that time, even though he was ill enough that I did all the driving, we still hoped that he would improve.

Sunday, November 10, 2019

Tom had two daughters from a previous marriage but had totally lost all contact with one of them. His younger daughter, Amy, was married to John and they had three talented sons, Caison, Christian and Keller. Tom loved those grandsons, even though his time with them was limited.

We had one son, Ben.

In 2014, Ben married his high school sweetheart, Emily, at the Huguenot Church. We were all so happy and loved her family. He finished seminary in Louisville at Louisville Presbyterian Theological Seminary, and then they moved to Athens for her to attend vet school at UGA. After three years in Athens, she told him that she wanted a divorce, that she was gay. This was June 2019.

Tom had definitely gone downhill by this time, and Ben had been coming home every few weeks to have time with his dad. Ben had a good job and thought he had a good, happy life, so this announcement from Emily blindsided him. He quit his job, moved home and helped me care for his dad for the next four months. He got an apartment for himself and Rascal, but spent the days at our house. Deep grief had touched our family. Tom was distraught for Ben, as was I, and the pain was almost more than any of us could bear. The timing was awful, but it did give Ben unlimited time with his dad.

Grief from a broken marriage. A mother watching her son grieve over a young marriage that dissolved, through no fault of his, nor without any choice being given. Another BAM, it's over and I want a divorce. A new life to build while having to find a new job, a new place to live, a dying father, a broken mother. Grief that moves through the same stages that we read about from a death, although the anger was very slow to emerge. A minister friend who had traveled the same road told Ben it was ok to be angry, it was a necessary step. The pain, the lack of self-confidence, the loss of a vision for his life, the loss of a planned future, the loss of a best friend to walk the next few months with. This is grief. A dead marriage.

Monday, November 11, 2019

Another strategy for dealing with this pain is to update/upgrade the house. Many projects were ignored due to Tom's illness. I had a living room chair that he'd basically lived in for two years recovered. That lead to a different color rug. That led to getting rid of a green upholstered rocking chair and ottoman. That left a space, so ordered a small recliner. Ordered a large rug for that room.

Ben used his time and updated light switches and inside ceiling lights. He also changed out the outside lanterns. They had all been in the house for over thirty years, so the replacements were not only new and clean, but provided a lift emotionally.

This took time and energy and provided a distraction. Ben continued to job hunt and I continued to clean out. Wish I had some way to help with his pain.

Tuesday, November 12, 2020

I tried to coax a close minister friend to tell me what happens after we die, knowing that he didn't and couldn't have the answers. One of the things most absent to me is Tom's arms around me. I just wanted reassurance that my husband would hold me again, and of course that was not my friend's assurance to offer. I think of that daily. What does happen when one dies? Will we be together again? Will we recognize each other and still love? So many questions and no answers. I dwell on that too much, I think. But how can I not?

Wednesday, November 13, 2019

I continue to clean out drawers and cabinets. Donated a lot of his medical supplies that were unopened to a company who would accept them. Finding the right organization takes time also. Took all of his old meds to a disposal site.

A friend brought dinner over and we sat and talked for hours. Tom had conducted her second marriage a few short years ago and it had been really special to see them so happy.

Thursday, November 14, 2019

I have placed new pictures around the house in every room except the bathroom (and that may be next) of him, of us, of our family. It gives me a quick sense of peace, brings a smile to my face and makes me feel he is present. This may not help everyone, but it helps me.

I am also so lucky to have recordings of his sermons on the church website. I have written copies in a file cabinet, but to be able to hear his voice is such a gift. Often when I get into bed at night, I listen to a sermon, to be comforted by his voice. What a voice it was too. I heard it said that he could read the telephone book and people would listen!

One night, I was listening to a sermon and Barkley left her bed, walked to his side of the bed, walked into the guest room and Ben's old room. She finally settled in the hall. I believe that she was looking for him, as she had heard his voice.

When he was in the hospital for six weeks, they actually allowed me to take Barkley to see him for a visit. They had a special relationship.

Friday, November 15, 2019

I have begun going through boxes of old papers and files and cleaning out. He was such a pack rat. I have recycled, shredded, organized to keep, saved for Amy and for Ben, cried and laughed. It makes me feel so close to him to see his handwriting, to read his words.

Several things I have come across I have mailed to the persons that the correspondence was to or from (these were his copies). People seem to be touched by this gesture and have responded.

I mailed a large box to his best friend in North Carolina containing a script that Steve had written and asked Wendell to proof, letters, information and pictures from their two trips to Russia, a couple of sweater vests and a couple of books.

Saturday, November 16, 2019

I have learned to make a playlist on Spotify and I add songs that make me laugh, make me cry, and some just good old beach music. I listen to music a lot when I am alone, which is basically all day. For years, with my husband's profound hearing loss, listening to music in the home or in the car was too difficult to deal with, so we stopped. I have missed the music and it is a good thing to reenter my world.

Sunday, November 17, 2019

Just couldn't face church again. Ben and I met friends for lunch. One of the gentlemen has lost two wives. He understands. He gets it.

He told me that his children from his first wife told him that they felt that he was grieving more for his second wife than he had for their mom. The reality, as he explained it, was that when his first wife died, he was working full time running a company, he had two children, he was trying to regroup from Hurricane Hugo and reopen the business. We all knew how much he loved her, needed her, depended on her. He still to this day peppers his conversation with, "She said," referring to her, his first wife. But the kids felt a different grief.

Monday, November 18, 2019

For years, these days in November brought a trip for our family to the American Speech and Hearing Convention. I was fortunate to be in a position that paid my expenses, and Tom would arrange his academic calendar and syllabi so he could also go. We took Ben out of school and the three of us flew to Anaheim, Seattle, Boston, Orlando, New Orleans, San Francisco, DC, and San Antonio among other places. What great trips! While I was in courses, Tom and Ben explored the area and then we all had dinner together and all day Saturday together. Our friend Mitch was around for these also and frequently joined in on our excursions. These are wonderful memories. It's amazing what a time of year, or a season, can make you reflect upon.

Tuesday, November 19, 2019

More to-do things. Got Ben's name on safety deposit box.

Wednesday, November 20, 2019

Today is Dad's birthday. He would have been ninety-eight years old.

Grief varies of course with the individual and the circumstances. I was twenty-eight when my dad died. He played golf the day before, and we had a big family dinner on Sunday to celebrate my younger sister's pregnancy. He went to bed early that night after telling my mom that he didn't feel great. He never got up. He died from a massive coronary. He was fifty-eight years old. That shock, that unexpected death, rocked my world. My dad loved his three girls and he was our strength. But, for me, that grief translated into energy to care for our mom. I was the one in town with power of attorney, etc. Every day I would leave work at NCSD, and go straight to Mom's house, to be with her, to help in any way that I could. Sometimes I would find her on the floor, sobbing. I missed Dad and I needed him, but I had a supportive husband who was a good man, and he and his wonderful family helped me. I had a full-time job. I had a home to take care of and groceries to buy. I had a busy life. Grief over Dad came in moments of driving up the driveway to Mom's house and automatically looking to see if Dad was sitting on the front porch. Hearing something and thinking, "I can't wait to tell Dad this." I actually remember our last conversation. He called me that Sunday afternoon and said, "Five ACC teams made the NCAA tournament! Bye!" Moments like that. Also, the feeling that my "protector" was gone. Busyness is good. Being needed is good.

Thursday, November 21, 2019

I have a friend whose husband died of cancer, leaving her with two young children. Prepared—possibly. Devastated—absolutely. Scared—without a doubt. She had no choice but to keep moving for her children. She told me after Tom died that she had a friend who would pick her up in the car and drive around and let her scream and cry. A friend who was there at any time.

She has paid that back with me. She takes me to lunch, and listens. She answers my texts and makes me laugh.

Friday, November 22, 2019

I move through the days, completing mundane tasks, continuing to go through papers. I cry. I'm filled with a loss that I have never felt before. The questions arise… "What if I had done this? Why wasn't I a better wife or lover? How did we waste time being angry or sad?" I fluctuate between despair of what all I did wrong and delight of all that we did right. We were faithful, we loved, we had a son together, we traveled some and laughed some. We supported each other through some horrendous times and never stopped loving each other. So why do I despair? Is any marriage perfect? Why isn't he here to talk with me and to hold my hand? Why was I so lucky to have found him, then lost him? Why? Why? Why?

Is this a mental illness? Is this normal?

Saturday, November 23, 2019

Another football Saturday. Watched the games, but something is missing. We did this together. We planned our days or evenings around the games. He introduced me to Clemson, and I introduced him to Carolina. We attended a few games over the years in both Clemson and in Chapel Hill, more of course while Ben was in school at Clemson, but we never had season tickets. Our game time was mainly at home, watching on tv, and we loved that.

I remember when Clemson won the national championship in 2016. We celebrated with neighbors (Clemson neighbors) toasting the victory. Boy, was Tom happy!!

That was the same year that the Tarheels won the NCAA basketball tournament and the Cubs won the World Series! So glad that we experienced that year together! Our three teams in one year!

Sunday, November 24, 2019

The Huguenot Church had not really made Advent a part of their Christmas season until my husband arrived. He purchased an Advent wreath, added greenery and Advent candles, wrote Advent readings for the four Sundays and Christmas Eve, placed inserts in the bulletins to explain the various Chrismons and supported me in my quest to get a Chrismon tree. The women of the church paid for me to purchase a tall fake tree. I organized persons in the church to cross-stitch Chrismons and provided them patterns, thread, hoops, scissors and encouragement. Tom and I framed each one as they were returned, and then before the first Sunday in Advent, we decorated the Chrismon tree and he set up the Advent wreath. We did this annually for eight years with the help of various church members.

So, here it is. The last Sunday before Advent begins. Just couldn't face church again but wanted to be a part of the wreath and tree, so Ben and I met Woody and Kristen for lunch after church, and the four of us decorated. There is a committee to decorate the church with wreaths and greenery, and it is always beautiful.

We got it done, and I am glad that we did. Tom would have liked that.

We had also begun the tradition of an annual devotional booklet written by members of the congregation. Woody took it over this year and asked me to write one. This is what I wrote:

HOPE

The wolf and the lamb shall feed together, the lion shall eat straw like the ox...They shall not hurt or destroy on all my holy mountain, says the Lord. Isaiah 65:25 (NRSV)

HOPE, I said out loud after reading the email from Woody asking me to write a devotional about hope... Wow, I thought. My husband is critically ill, my son's world has been torn apart, I am holding on by a thread...Hope?

My thoughts quickly changed to "Get over yourself girl!" If we have no hope, what do we have? The world is so much larger than my small corner.

There is hope for an illness to improve, hope for a love to appear, hope for world peace, hope for people to come together to address the climate crisis, hope for all children to live in safety. So many, many hopes that give us courage to fight, to give, to dream.

Mary had hope that Joseph would stay by her side. The shepherds had hope when the angel appeared. The wise men had hope when they followed a star.

So, in this season of joy, peace, and love, the first is hope.

My hope and my prayer, is that the people of the world find a way to reach out to each other in love, and work together to save the Earth. My hope is for the children of the world to grow up in a place where they can learn, and laugh and sing and love.

Our Father, we are grateful for the gift of hope. Help us to share this gift with others during this season and all through the year. AMEN

Monday, November 25, 2019

After working this a.m., Ben and I met Stuart and Susan and Mitch for lunch. Friends continue to make contact, reserve time for us and do kind things for us.

Made the first of the fall's pumpkin bread. I usually make forty-plus loaves during the season. Tom loved it so much!

Tuesday, November 26, 2019

Cleaned out our bathroom drawers and painted them. They had not been painted since we bought the house twenty-six years ago, so they needed it.

Took Barkley to Johns Island to a friend's house who is keeping her while we are gone for Thanksgiving.

Wednesday, November 27, 2019

Ben and I drove to Florida to Tom's sister's house for Thanksgiving. We'd had long discussions about what to do for the holiday.

Thanksgiving at our home was a big deal, much as it is in many homes. We typically had seventeen to twenty people, played corn hole, had the fire pit going, fried the turkey outside, ate too much, played games afterwards and just had time together. Most of the friends who came were the same annually. Emily's parents and sisters had come for many years, even during their dating years. Her grandparents from Michigan came one year. So that is five fewer people, plus the pain of Ben's first Thanksgiving without Emily. Tom's best friend, Steve, and his family came every year from North Carolina.

No Tom, no Bousers. He and Steve had been celebrating Thanksgivings together longer than Brenda and I had been in the picture, so a long tradition. Sometimes the Revelise family joined us too.

So, we decided trying to reconstruct Thanksgiving at our house was off for at least this year.

What to do? We talked and decided to see if we could go to Aunt June's. She is Tom's older sister and was unable to travel to Charleston for his service due to illness. She lives alone, but near her son and his family, which is why she moved to Florida.

They graciously agreed for us to come. June had been like a grandmother to Ben, and we both loved her a lot. It was a way for us to grieve together.

So, Ben and I left for Florida.

Thursday, November 28, 2019

Thanksgiving Day in Florida. A very different day, but one that I think meant a lot to June. Her son and his family brought Thanksgiving dinner from Publix, and we all ate together. They stayed a few hours and we talked and visited. Monty and June pulled out some photo albums to share with us, many of which were pictures of Wendell growing up with Buddy and June. It was a good visit.

The room that I slept in had a framed picture of Wendell with his siblings and his mom after his dad died. I had never seen it, but June gave it to me. That night looking at that picture, I felt like he was in the room with me.

Friday, November 29, 2019

Spent the day driving home. I hate I-95 but Ben did all the driving coming home.

Saturday, November 30, 2019

Amy, John and the boys came over for brunch. Ben made waffles and, man, can those boys eat! It was good to see them. I had boxes of pictures and other things that I had been through and saved for them to have of Tom's. I think it meant a lot to them. I had found things that Amy gave or made him when she was a little girl and some other things of his that they wanted.

Really good for me to have this time with his daughter and her family. Sometimes, I can feel him smiling.

Sunday, December 1, 2019

First Sunday in Advent. I did go to church. Cried again, but I made it. Advent was Tom's favorite time in the church year to preach. I knew this and missed him even more. His presence is so strong at the church. His name on the list of pastors, the Advent wreath, his name on people's lips.

Monday, December 2, 2019

I have another, older friend who has been a widow for many years. When I emailed her that I was trying to write as a means of therapy, she sent me this email:

> *Don't sugarcoat anything you write. I had a friend whose husband died. They had 3 small boys. She told me she got so frustrated one day she yelled out and said to no one In particular "oh Smitty I hate you for leaving me to raise these boys". I asked her if it helped her. She said it did after she cried and said a prayer. Sometimes you have to have a little temper tantrum and let off a little steam even if it is aimed at GOD. He knows why you did. I used to say everyone ought to have a little red in their hair. Go yell at someone. I love you bunches.*

I love her too!

Tuesday, December 3, 2019

Took a chair to be recovered. It was a green chair with a green ottoman. We had already had it recovered once, as we had owned the chair for a long time. It was in a reading corner in the living room with a lamp and nestled in front of the floor-to-ceiling bookcases that Tom built. He read the newspaper there every morning, and for the past two years spent many of his waking moments there, reading, napping, visiting. It was in bad shape, so I picked out some new material and took it to be recovered.

I feel guilty, but think he would be ok with it. The green had to go, so I turned to a blue (which meant the green rug had to go).

As I write this months later, I suddenly realize that now I sit and read the newspaper there every morning.

Wednesday, December 4, 2019

Still working. Doing Christmas language activities with the kids. Might be the highlight of Christmas this year.

Thursday, December 5, 2019

For several years, Wendell and I enjoyed attending the Creche Festival at Mepkin Abbey. We would drive the forty-five minutes through the national forest and spend a delightful hour or two at Mepkin. As a professor, he had taken multiple classes there to listen to the monks, to tour, to learn about their faith. He had developed a friendship with some of them.

One of his former students had written me after Tom's death and had mentioned that "Dr. Guerry introduced me to Mepkin Abbey."

The Creche Festivals were fun and interesting. The level of creativity amazed us.

So, this year, Francie, my walking friend and neighbor, went with me. She had never been. It was fun to introduce it to someone new, but again Tom's presence was there. I had never been to Mepkin without him. We had been there for Piccolo Spoleto concerts and other events in addition to the Creche Festival.

Is he everywhere I am? Is this feeling going to last? I hope so.

Took Ben to the airport to fly to Mexico for a music concert. He had already paid for it and would lose the money if he did not go, so he went and met two friends there. I think he needs some kind of pick-me-up right now.

Friday, December 6, 2019

And speaking of memories and of Tom, every year since we were dating, we attended the library book sale in October. He was usually one of the first in line on Friday mornings, and then he went again with me on Saturday. He brought boxes of books home. Have I mentioned that he was a true bibliophile? Anyway, the event was marked on our calendars as soon as it was announced.

So, I went to a smaller version of that one with Francie.

Saturday, December 7, 2019

A few years ago, my friend Sylvia and I started a tradition of walking King Street one Saturday in December. We would window-shop, browse, eat lunch, have a drink and chat. Today was the day.

But I bought a couch! Other than his piano, the sunroom had been empty since the hospital bed had been removed. So, I bought a couch on sale to have a small conversation area in the sunroom. Amy has his organ that had been in there, and Ben had taken the wicker furniture, so there was space.

Sunday, December 8, 2019

Actually, made church again. Second Sunday in Advent.

Monday, December 9, 2019

Today is my younger sister's birthday and my ex-husband's also. She is deaf and the reason that I followed the professional track that I did. She has been wonderful to me through all of this, with frequent texts, emails and pictures of her cats. I am lucky to have my sisters.

Samp has also reached out to me. He happily remarried many years ago, but he has remained a friend. I'm lucky for that reason too.

Tuesday, December 10, 2019

I love to read. Tom and I shared books and talked about books, and both of us were prolific readers prior to falling in love.

Books have been a help to me during this time. Some I read to escape, other I read for a desire to find someone who has walked this path and has put their feelings into words. A friend suggested *Grief* by CS Lewis. I read it, and parts were meaningful to me and I could relate. Lewis wrote this book after his wife had died.

My sister gave me *The Cure for Sorrow* by Jan Richardson. This is a book of blessings for times of grief. Again, some of her words really spoke to me, perhaps because she too had lost her husband.

I found one of Tom's books called *Light from Many Lamps* by Lillian Eichler Watson. It was given to him in appreciation for having led a study series and inscribed with these words:

"Thanks, Wendell, for Light shared with us in Lexington." It is a compilation of many authors' writings about varied emotions. I really found parts of it very helpful and even ordered one for a friend whose mom is dying.

The pattern that I have developed is to read a few pages in these kinds of books every night when I get into bed. Then I read my Baldacci, Grisham, Grippando kind of book.

However, my greatest comfort continues in reading Tom's words. Sometimes I just sit and read old cards that he gave me through the years. Contact with him is what I crave.

Wednesday, December 11, 2019

Took my annual batch of pumpkin bread to MSA. Nice to share with folks and everyone loves it!

Christmas is coming. It has always been a favorite holiday of mine for so many reasons. Tom did a sermon one time and mentioned the grief that I displayed on the 26th every year when it was all over. It's hard to even think of Christmas this year.

Thursday, December 12, 2019

Today would have been Mom and Dad's sixty-seventh wedding anniversary.

Ben and I talked about Christmas. He suggested no presents and no stockings but that he did want to decorate.

So, decorate we did.

Two trees, candles in the windows, wreath on the door. Since we bought this house, twenty-six years ago, we have had two trees. Our regular family tree is in the living room. A smaller tree with white lights graces the foyer. This is where we hung the wooden Chrismons that Tom made. Very simple, but lovely.

For many years we hosted a Christmas Eve brunch. We typically had forty to fifty persons, all families that we were close to. Each year, Tom would give a Chrismon to each family.

So many of those families have contacted me this year to mention hanging their Chrismons and thinking about Tom.

Friday, December 13, 2019

Linda was a high school friend, a college roommate, and one of the very best friends that I have in the world today. She flew from Seattle to Charleston to be with me during those days after Tom's death. She talked with me, cried with me, laughed with me and drank wine with me. I needed her desperately and she was here. Through the ensuing months, Linda has stayed in touch at least weekly by phone, text, cards, gifts (a beautiful candle) and always with a way of saying, "I'm thinking about you and I love you."

During one of those conversations, she mentioned that she would like to talk with me sometime about my dad's death and how it had affected me. This gave me pause to stop and remember that Linda and her family were grieving too. I have pondered that request for a while now, and even though we have not had the conversation (we are waiting for a face-to-face and a bottle of wine), I want to share some of my thoughts. I have no revelations. I believe that each individual who dies and each person who loved and mourns them is unique. There are no guidelines, no script. Linda and Karen and Tommy face each day grieving for their dad in very different ways. Donna, Terri and I grieved for our parents in very different ways. What is comfort to one may be meaningless to another.

Perhaps my thoughts are that one should grieve in the way that best meets your needs. No one and no book can dictate how you should grieve. Remembering that our parents were human, and just like us, they made mistakes in parenting and in life. God knows I did. If you are fortunate enough to have a spouse or a partner or a friend or a minister that you can talk to, do it. Share the questions and the bad memories. Talk through them. Share the questions and the good memories. Talk through them. Hopefully the good memories of a parent who loved us, cared for us, was there for us, had fun with us, challenged us, took pride in us, will surpass any other memories. Unfortunately, not all of us have those good memories to fall back on.

Saturday, December 14, 2019

A quiet Saturday. I am enjoying looking at the tree lights. They have always been one of my favorite things about the holidays, especially with all the other lights off.

We enjoyed an annual family tradition of "sleeping under the tree" one night during the season. All three of us would pile on the floor, leave the tree lights on all night and enjoy the lights and the fire. This is a tradition that I am guessing Ben will continue. It was fun!

Looking at the mantle with four stockings hung (the two dogs each have one) is another constant reminder. Last year there were seven.

Should we have hung Tom's? They are all going to be empty so not sure why we didn't.

Sunday, December 15, 2019

Today was Lessons and Carols at church, one of my favorite services of the year. I was asked to be a reader. Several people mentioned that they were concerned that I would not get through it, but I did.

This afternoon we had a new, special service. Woody put it together and it was titled "Blue Christmas." It was for persons struggling, perhaps with grief, perhaps pain about something else. It was a small crowd, around twenty persons, but an incredibly meaningful service. We lit candles and prayed and sat in silence. A chili and cornbread supper was provided afterwards.

Woody used the analogy of "an empty chair." He actually placed one of the pulpit chairs near where he was speaking to illustrate the point. For most people there, I imagine it was just that, an analogy. For Ben and for me, it was much more. That was Tom's chair. He had sat there almost every Sunday for eight years.

Monday, December 16, 2019

Christmas is fast approaching. What will we do? The two of us cannot just sit here and look at each other all day. I am glad we decided no presents. Ben is still not working, and neither of us need anything that money can buy. We discuss Christmas Day, much as we did Thanksgiving.

We decide to try and volunteer somewhere that might help others, and might keep us busy. I emailed organizations and waited for responses. This late, many told me that they were already full.

But I did hear from the Lodge House. This is a home for cancer patients while they receive treatment at MUSC. They do want us Christmas Day to help. This is a good thing.

Tuesday, December 17, 2019

Sometimes it is easier to say, "I am fine," than it is to say, "I'm falling apart."

Wednesday, December 18, 2019

Our annual neighborhood party is tonight. Everyone brings a dish and we share a meal. Last year Tom was too ill to go but insisted that I go. He always prayed, so the minister's wife prayed since he was not there. This year, I told them I would come IF I did not have to pray, and also that Ben did not have to either. They agreed.

We went and Ben actually thought it was fun. We have good neighbors.

Thursday, December 19, 2019

One game I play privately is lines from songs that had meaning to us. Some of my favorites:

Took the hand of a preacher man and we made love in the sun

I remember our first embrace and the smile that was on your face

You turned my life around

I'll be your friend, and I'll be your lover

Don't it make my brown eyes blue

Loving you was easier than anything I'll ever do again

These make me smile.

Friday, December 20, 2019

Alone, alone with my thoughts and my nightmares and my good dreams. Alone with my music and alone with our dog. No, my dog. That's another thing, when do you change the pronouns?

Saturday, December 21, 2019

Getting very close to Christmas. I understand for the very first time why some people don't like, or don't get excited about the holidays. It's not the time to be alone. One is supposed to be happy and excited and full of anticipation. I feel empty.

Sunday, December 22, 2019

Finished delivering all the pumpkin bread. At least that was normal.
Doing no Christmas baking for our home this year, and for the first
time in my adult life, I did not send cards.

Monday, December 23, 2019

After more than two months, I finally have an appointment with the Social Security office. Most was done over the phone, but they said that I had to have a face-to-face to get death benefits. They told me to bring several things, including the death certificate. Ben goes with me and we take all the papers, pull a number and wait. After perhaps twenty minutes, they call my number. Finished in ten minutes. Something else to check off the list.

Tuesday, December 24, 2019

Christmas Eve. Another difficult first. Last year this time, Tom had conducted both candlelight services himself as Phil had his second stroke. We have some beautiful pictures that were taken by an Elder from the balcony.

But this year, as with everything else, all is different. I considered not going, but I wanted to go, wanted to worship, and no other church would be the same. So, Ben and I and a friend of his went. The service was beautiful as always. It was incredibly sad for me though, and there were multiple times the tears were streaming. During the singing of Silent Night was one of those times.

I had made reservations for dinner, and the three of us ate at Poogan's Porch. Even that was filled with memories, as I had told Tom on the porch of Poogan's that we were having a baby. Poogan's was our special restaurant when we were dating and an easy walk from my apartment. I would not have selected it for tonight though, as there were just too many emotions inside me, but I was able to get reservations.

Christmas Day, 2019

I think that this was the first time in my life that I have awakened to an empty house on Christmas morning. I started a fire, fixed some coffee, ate a country ham biscuit and settled in with home movies. I watched for two hours. It made me feel closer to Tom, to Mom, and brought back so many good memories.

Ben came and we headed downtown to the Lodge House. We didn't know what to expect. As it turned out, they did not need us to help prepare Christmas dinner for the residents, as most had gone home. We ended up spending several hours cleaning out and rearranging the kitchen, a pantry and a storage closet. Hopefully it helped. We met a nice couple who are Jewish and who volunteer every Christmas Day so the staff can be off. People helping people.

After cleaning up and cooking our part of the meal, we headed to Donna and Carl's for dinner with their family. They were all there except for Kate. It was really good to be included, to see those grandkids of theirs, and to laugh. We were grateful.

We got through the day.

Thursday, December 26, 2019

No let-down from Christmas being over this year. More like relief.

The Rogers family came over for brunch. I had filled a brown grocery bag for each of the boys with things of their grandfather's. Things like hats, flashlights, books, a chalice. They seemed to enjoy going through their bags.

Friday, December 27, 2019

Watched the Tarheels play in their bowl game. We won.

Saturday, December 28, 2019

Watched the Clemson bowl game. We won.

Sunday, December 29, 2019

Five years ago, today, our family was preparing for Ben and Emily's wedding. We were all so very excited. The rehearsal dinner was to be held at 44 Queen in the courtyard, and it was an oyster roast/pig pick-in. The weather was awful, very cold and raining, so we moved what we could inside. Clemson was playing Oklahoma, so some friends kept us informed as to the score. Tom wrote them a beautiful poem, which we framed and gave to them later.

All that is to say, that in addition to dealing with the loss of his father, Ben is dealing with the loss of his wife as well. Getting through these firsts is very difficult. I wish I could help, but words cannot take away the pain…I know.

Monday, December 30, 2019

Brenda called a few weeks ago and offered to get tickets to the UNC basketball game in Chapel Hill. She remembered the wedding date and that this would have been Ben and Emily's fifth anniversary. She thought it might be easier on Ben to be out of town. I agreed, as did he, so the tickets were purchased.

Monday a.m. we drove to Chapel Hill. Ben has always been good company and the trip was fun. We got to Chapel Hill in time for lunch, walked around campus, went to Johnny T-shirt and just enjoyed ourselves. He has a little blue blood in that orange body of his.

We met our friends, including their daughter, Kate, and a friend of hers for dinner. Then we took buses to the Dean Dome and watched the Heels win. (Horrible season, so glad they won that one.) Ben had never been to the Dean Smith Center, so it was a good experience for him.

I think it was a good choice for keeping him distracted from the anniversary and I remain grateful to the Bousers for their thoughtfulness.

Tuesday, December 31, 2019

Drove home from Southern Pines where we had spent the night.

Ben and I are both ready to be finished with 2019 and praying that 2020 will be a year of healing and happiness.

Wednesday, January 1, 2020

A new tradition. We decided to have a few folks over for a New Year's lunch. Did a pork tenderloin, hoppin john, collards and cornbread. A few neighbors and friends came. It was good.

Thursday, January 2, 2020

Somedays I wake up to the reality that this is not a dream and I feel like screaming. I want explanations, understanding, comprehension, companionship, him.

Speaking of yelling, I have done that too. I was driving to work one day, crossing the Ravenel Bridge, listening to Christmas music. A familiar song was playing, and they pronounced a word differently than I had ever heard. I thought, well who is right? Then it started, "Damn it, Wendell Guerry! (He was always Wendell Guerry when he was in trouble!) I need to ask you a question and you are not even here to answer it." The tears, the yelling, the cussing—not a great idea on the Ravenel! The so unexpected responses to the prosaic.

Friday, January 3, 2020

Ben and I undecorate. Always a difficult day, but not as much this year. Packing the ornaments away, just like hanging them, brought a flood of memories of where we'd gotten them. On every trip, small and large, we always found a Christmas shop and purchased an ornament. Our tree was not fancy, nor themed, but it was full of memories.

Saturday, January 4, 2020

I think that I have made enough progress with the papers and files that I can begin on the books. Have I mentioned that he loved books? We have thousands of books in this house, many on floor-to-ceiling bookcases that he built in several rooms. There are also books in boxes stacked to the ceiling in the study and boxes of books in the attic.

This is going to be a project.

Sunday, January 5, 2020

We stopped going to movies years ago as it was both expensive and difficult with his hearing loss. Even with the infrared systems, it was difficult.

Today, Sylvia and I went to a movie, *Little Women*! What a relaxing distraction. Good to have girlfriends to do things with.

Monday, January 6, 2020

Finished putting away the last of the Christmas stuff. Ben and I managed to downsize quite a bit and to reduce the number of bins returning to the attic. Wendell always did this. I took down and he carefully packed away and labeled each bin.

He loved labels! We have found laughter in so many things, including his label habit. We even found clear bins of wine corks given to him to make trivets that were labeled.

Tuesday, January 7, 2020

Back at work after a few weeks off. Good to see the kids and to be doing therapy again. My happy place.

But my comfort place is our home. At home I feel surrounded by him, pictures of him, furniture that he made, pieces that he refinished, chairs that he caned, books that he loved, Home.

Wednesday, January 8, 2020

Drove to Wilmington to spend a couple of nights with Linda. She is there for a few weeks before returning to Seattle. John is already in Seattle and back at work.

Thursday, January 9, 2020

The time with Linda is so good for me. She lets me cry and talk about Tom all that I want. She makes me laugh. She shares her life, good times and bad. Somehow, I can let down with her. With Ben, I can be honest and talk, but I am constantly wanting to build him up, not to make him worry about me.

Linda and I had dinner with her ninety-three-year-old mother. Amazing lady.

Friday, January 10, 2020

Drove home. I don't like being in the car alone. I used to not mind it, maybe it is age. Maybe I am just alone too much.

Saturday, January 11, 2020

Maybe I should explain the Wendell/Tom name exchange just in case someone ever reads this. My husband was named Wendell Thomas Guerry. He grew up being called Wendell but had always hated his name. When he returned home to Charleston, he wanted to be called Tom. His dad, who was known as Tom, had died. So many of our friends and colleagues got to know him as Tom. Other people, family members, who had known him as Wendell, stuck with that. I was for the most part, able to refer to him depending on who we were with. There were occasions, however, when we had people around of mixed company, and this story inevitably came up. He hated that story and said he never should have changed his name, but he did.

Sunday, January 12, 2020

I am getting ready to have four rooms painted in the house, so spent the day in preparation.

Monday, January 13, 2020

After work, trying to stay out of the painters' way. Good time to make some headway with these books.

Clemson National Championship game on tonight. We lost.

Tuesday, January 14, 2020

Painters still here.

Tom had started an online bookselling business a few years back. It has been inactive since our Boston trip, as he never reopened it. So, I reopened it and went through each listed book to be sure that I still had it.

Now I am going through the boxes of books. I enter the information into the computer and see if it is worth listing to sell. If so, it goes on a specific shelf. If not, it goes into a box to go to Goodwill or to the library book sale.

Wednesday, January 15, 2020

Forever the pragmatist, to a fault, would be one of the ways to describe me. Growing up, I never dreamed of being a mom, was never a babysitter, etc., but being a mom is one of the two best things in my life. Not a good visionary. When our son, who was in seminary, decided not to pursue a career in ministry, my left brain said, "But if you go to seminary, that's what you do. What kind of job will you be trained for?" My husband, the right brain, visionary minister said, "A seminary education is worth so much in life. Follow your heart."

I write all of this to say, now Ms. Practical…is having some doubts.

The first "event" occurred when I opened my Spotify one day and a song that I had never played nor added to my playlist was playing. I was familiar with it, Bette Midler's "Wind Beneath My Wings." The words were familiar also in that I had used them in a letter to my husband in February 2019 in a memory book that I had put together, "A Life of Ministry," for his eightieth birthday. He had also used the words in his last sermon, June 2019. Those lyrics had meaning to **US.** Was he reaching out to me?

Thursday, January 16, 2020

Took six boxes of books to Goodwill. They are either going to love me or hate me when this is over.

Friday, January 17, 2020

Had lunch with Francie at the Grits Counter. Boy, was it good!!
Friends have no idea how much they help.

Saturday, January 18, 2020

Donna and Carl, Ben and I watched the Heels on TV and ate lunch together. We lost.

Fun to be with them though.

Sunday, January 19, 2020

Went to church. Phil preaching. It is getting easier, and it is where I want to be on Sunday mornings. There is a need there.

Monday, January 20, 2020

Ben has a job! Thank goodness as I think this will be a step towards healing.

Tuesday, January 21, 2020

But back to the unknown. For months and for hundreds of hours, I have been going through books and papers. Having completed (kind of) the study boxes, I started getting boxes out of the attic. Having done maybe twenty-five or so boxes, I got into bed one night. Clear as a bell Wendell says, "You are going to get spider bitten if you keep putting your hands in those boxes." So, the very next morning, I am back at my task. I enter the attic and gingerly remove a box to the study. I sit down, open the box, and there is a spider!! The first one I have seen. Explain

Wednesday, January 22, 2020

The painters are finished. What a lighter, cleaner look. Glad to have that done.

Still a Wendell Guerry home though, something that I would never, ever change. A friend walked in our house one time (the third house that we had bought together) and remarked that every house that we lived in looks like Wendell. I'm glad. Just one of many reasons why I don't want to sell and move. This was our home. I can repaint, upholster furniture, get rid of a few old pieces that we purchased and still leave it as our home. I think he would like the changes, except for the beadboard in the powder room downstairs. He put that up and it was natural wood. I had it painted white…

Thursday, January 23, 2020

The sofa was delivered today for the sunroom. This was the one I purchased on my King Street day with Sylvia. How perfect was the timing with the painters finished in the sunroom!

I mailed a letter of resignation to the home health agency that contracts with me to see adult stroke patients and swallowing patients. I just do not have it in me to do this anymore. I actually thought when Hospice was with Tom that I might want to work with Hospice and do swallowing assessments and try to make a person's last time on earth a little easier.

What was I thinking?

Friday, January 24, 2020

One day seems much like another. I do miss our time together, just talking. For years, we had our own happy hour where he would have a glass of red wine and I would have a glass of white. This is when we talked about our days. We talked about world events. We talked about our family. We talked.

Saturday, January 25, 2020

Ben liking his job. Right now, he is off weekends, which is nice, but when promoted, he will work weekends.

Sunday, January 26, 2020

I went to church. Woody preaching. I feel good when I am there, as it seems right. Hard to break old habits, and there were very few Sundays in our marriage, and indeed in my life, that I have not been in church.

After church, Wendell and I would always eat lunch out. It was a time for him to relax, regroup, and look forward to his afternoon nap.

Monday, January 27, 2020

Somehow, I manage to stay busy. With work, sorting books, housework, dogs (I have two during the days), and reading, I manage to pass the days. I think staying busy is the key. Not a TV watcher except for movies and games. Ben has introduced me to some sitcoms such as *Parks and Rec* and *Schitt's Creek*, which we watch during our dinner. My TV is not on during the day though. I wish I was still able to cross-stitch, but the eyes can't handle it.

Tuesday, January 28, 2020

Had breakfast out with two friends from the church. These ladies have been so good to me, and it is good to have someone to eat breakfast with.

Wednesday, January 29, 2020

Had the chimney inspected and they found cracks. Seems that if we want to use the fireplace (and we are major fire burners), that the repair is going to be about $5,000. Eek! Now in the past, Tom and I would discuss this. He would ponder it, I would say, "Well we have to do it." Some household decisions are easier to make on one's own, but this one...

Thursday, January 30, 2020

Well, today was a lot of fun. (Hard to convey sarcasm in print.) Had my physical for the insurance change. I know that the fact that my sisters both have heart problems that they have traced to our dad and maternal grandmother is going to be an issue. I explained to the lady that I had been tested for the same gene and that I don't have it. Gave her the name of the MD. Let's see how far that gets me.

I hate things like this, but I imagine most of us do.

Also, got the chimney repaired. Ouch!

Friday, January 31, 2020

I guess it is good that when you are living your lives, you don't dwell on your deaths. Sometimes I wish we had talked about it more, about one of us being alone. About what to do and how to do it.

This is foreign to anything that I have ever known or ever experienced. I think I was so busy throughout my adult life with family, work, church, volunteering, that I didn't take the time to think ahead, to have the discussions, to plan. Now all that I have are the reflections.

Saturday, February 1, 2020

When I went to work in the mornings before Tom died, I tried to arrange for friends to come by. Ben was available, but he also needed some time to job hunt, etc. Amy took off work a couple of days so that I could work. On this particular day, two friends of Tom were coming by. One is blind, one is the bionic man. While walking behind our couch, one of them managed to hit the glass door in the bookcase and break it. Tom told me later that they heard a noise but didn't know what it was.

Ben cleaned up the glass that had all fallen inside. I began to look for glass places that might fix it.

Today we drove up to see the model home where he is working and went to two glass places, neither of which was open.

I made it to church again.

Monday, February 3, 2020

Had lunch with Woody. Kristen couldn't make it. Sat and talked for a long long time about stuff. He is a good listener, and a good friend.

Sometimes I feel that I can't talk about anything except Tom when I have the opportunity. I have always considered myself a listener and could ask questions and draw people out so that they could talk. Now, I want to talk. But I don't want to either. Keeping my feelings inside keeps them mine.

There is nothing people can say. Nothing they can do. I have to do this. But I can't make it alright. It's never going to be alright. Woody lets me say all those things.

Tuesday, February 4, 2020

Ben and I had brunch at Page's. I love breakfast at Page's. Tom and I would go early about once a week during the week and get a good breakfast. Mine would last about four days as I only ate about a fourth of it. So good.

Wednesday, February 5, 2020

After making an appointment, Ben and I head to Summerville to select the stone for Tom's grave. I thought this would not be too bad, as it had been a while and we knew that he would have wanted something simple. I was wrong. Throughout the process, I could barely breathe.

The lady who worked there was kind, not pushy. She listened and did not draw out the process. She didn't even flinch when we asked for a Huguenot cross on the stone. We got through it, paid and were told it would be about three months.

Check off something else.

I think I had been dreading this as it just makes everything seem permanent. It is permanent, but this is kind of the last thing that I can do.

I hate this.

Why didn't we have a few more healthy years? What am I truly supposed to do now? Is there any reason for me to go on? I know I have Ben, and I do want to see him happy and with a partner who loves him. I know I have a fulfilling job that I love. I know I have friends and family who care and spend time with me. But I don't, nor will I ever, have Tom. I need his touch.

Thursday, February 6, 2020

For all the years of our marriage, Tom did our taxes or prepared everything to take to the accountant. All of the other finances, I did myself or we did together. I told him every year that all I knew about taxes was what he asked me to gather for him (my mileage, etc.). So here I am.

First question on the preparation form, married—Yes or No. Am I married? Wow, that hit hard. I feel married, but I don't think the IRS cares. So, first of many emails to the accountant. He says yes, you are married this year as we are filing jointly. Next year you will be single.

Spent hours trying to pull stuff together and compare to last year's return. Now I understand why Wendell always dreaded this.

Friday, February 7, 2020

Met a church friend for lunch. Good timing as the glass door was replaced and I could pick that up too.

Saturday, February 8, 2020

Another day with taxes. Books have been temporarily set aside.

Sunday, February 9, 2020

Sylvia went with me to church. It helps to have her with me.
We managed to have a good lunch afterwards too.

Monday, February 10, 2020

We are beginning to read about a new virus that began in China and is spreading around the world. We don't know what it will mean to us.

Tuesday, February 11, 2020

Ben has been replacing all of the old switch plates and outlets in the house, as well as some of the inside overhead lighting. Really helps to make things brighter as all were original to the house.

Wednesday, February 12, 2020

Continue to work two days per week. I am so grateful for this job. I love it and it is also a distraction and gives me a feeling of being needed. One would think that after being on call 24/7 for the past eighteen months, I would want to just chill. But that is the worst thing for me. This job keeps me focused and busy and constantly on my toes to learn a new therapy approach or work with a disability that I have not had much experience with.

Thursday, February 13, 2020

Had four SLP girlfriends over for a wine/appetizer/dinner night. Good to have people here. Everyone contributed to the meal and we laughed and talked. Yet, I was so glad when they left. I want people here, and I don't. Short time periods are about all that I am mentally capable of. Seems like it would be the opposite, that I would crave visits and time with friends. So much about this process that I do not understand.

Friday, February 14, 2020

Ben and I both ignoring Valentine's Day!

I asked Donna and Carl to come for lunch if Carl would look over my taxes to see if there are any glaring errors. They did and he was a huge help.

I think the taxes are ready to go!

Saturday, February 15, 2020

No more contacts. I did Google "communication with the deceased," and it appears to not be uncommon. One of the articles that I read said that most people say, "You are going to think I am crazy, but..." So, guess I am not unique in these happenings.

Sunday, February 16, 2020

Skipped church today. Did some reading.

Monday, February 17, 2020

Took the taxes downtown to David and had a nightmare experience. Took them in to give to the receptionist. She saw the name, expressed her condolences, then began to talk. And talk. And talk. For at least fifteen minutes she told me about her husband's death, how things never get better, how much support she had, and on and on. I could not believe it. I finally interrupted her and said, "I have to go!" Tears streaming down my face. She said, "Oh, I am so sorry." Walked to the parking lot and sat in the car and cried for a long time. What are people thinking? She did not mean to be unkind, but it was so very thoughtless. I pray that I never do that.

Hope I can answer David's questions when he calls or emails. I hate being alone and adulting alone.

Tuesday, February 18, 2020

Have been thinking about not signing my contract for next year. Is it right that I work another year? Should I hang it up? Do I have it in me? Can I give it up?

I have a meeting tomorrow morning with the principal, Dirk, to discuss this.

You know, it's a funny thing. People say, "You are so strong. You are doing great." You are torn between breaking down and saying, "You just don't know how frail I am," and straightening your back, putting your head up and plowing ahead. People see what they want to see, and it is much easier when someone is not falling apart in front of you. What choice do I have?

Wednesday, February 19, 2020

My meeting with Dirk was cancelled as he had a parent meeting. I began therapy, and what is typically a good morning was a great morning. I had fun, therapy was appropriate and successful, and I suddenly realized that I did not want to leave this job yet. I'm going to stay another year!

I have never liked the term "It's a God thing." My reasoning is that this is kind of pretentious

to assume that we know God did so and so or made so and so happen. But, whatever reason, I am glad that our meeting was cancelled!

Thursday, February 20, 2020

This virus keeps making headlines and is in the US now. Seattle seems to be the focal point and Linda and John are there. He is working from home and they are quarantined. Scary times.

Friday, February 21, 2020

Back to "events." I am going through an entire shelf of bound books that contain bulletins and church week writings from all the churches that Wendell served. I read everything that he had written, pondered it, tore out pages for recycling and book covers for trash. This one I kept. He began with these words, "Whenever a crisis comes, an opportunity is created." I found this and read it right at the beginning of the virus scare, when almost no one was taking it too seriously. I think he sent those words to me for encouragement

Saturday, February 22, 2020

Saturdays are hard days. Maybe because it is the weekend, and that's when you are planning and doing things. Maybe it's because everyone else is busy. I got lucky today. My wonderful niece Annie came over and we had a spinach salad and wine lunch. Better than that, we sat in the sunroom and talked for a couple of hours. It was a real gift to me. She has two young children and no time. When she suggested this, I was thrilled. I had not seen her since Christmas Eve at her parents' home when everyone was around so we had not had the opportunity to talk one-on-one.

Sunday, February 23, 2020

Made it to church. Woody preaching.

Monday, February 24, 2020

I think that the way that a parent dies, their health, their age, the circumstances, makes a huge difference in our acceptance of losing them. They will always be our mom or our dad, with all that entails, but dealing with their loss varies in the factors contributing to the loss.

Not really unlike how I am trying to deal with this recent grief. Not a perfect marriage, not a perfect man, but then he was married to a not-perfect woman. I have traveled the road of some bad memories, even had dreams about some of them. But I live in the memories of the good times, and the loving times.

Tuesday, February 25, 2020

There are times in our lives when we feel overwhelmed by all that life throws our way. It is in times like these that the support and love of the people around you make a difference. We never know what small gestures mean.

Wednesday, February 26, 2020

Is he contacting me? Am I just truly wanting that to be? I went searching one day for something in a hope chest in Ben's room and there on top were two wooden butterflies that he had made me years ago. Our romantic early years were entwined with butterflies and wildflowers, so these were very symbolic to me. But…they had already been there for many years.

Thursday, February 27, 2020

Amy's birthday, her first without her dad. I texted her and so did Ben.

Had lunch with Mitch at Angel Oak. I love that little restaurant on John's Island. Good to talk with Mitch. He gets it.

Ben and I had dinner with Elise. Always fun and good tacos!

Friday, February 28, 2020

I have always believed that you think of others, you try and help others, and you end up helping yourself. In taking on their pain, or sorrow, you give them part of yourself, but you get so much in return. Maybe it's an escape from your own problems or a refocus that takes away your pain, but it helps. I remember a sermon that Ben preached when in seminary about all of the mission trips that his youth group had taken in high school and the spring breaks in college when his group worked in NYC and other places. He said that they received so much more than they gave. In working in soup kitchens or replacing flooring or blowing insulation, they helped— yes. But, they learned about the world outside of their bubble and saw life through others' eyes.

Now, however, I can't seem to live that right now. My grief at times is so overwhelming that I don't think I can take another breath. It is so all consuming, so present. How do you deal with that? How do you recover or change your life plan, or get through another day?

Saturday, February 29, 2020

Ben and I voted today. First time to vote without Tom in thirty-three years.

Sunday, March 1, 2020

One of Tom's favorite hymns was "There's a Wideness in God's Mercy." He asked that it be sung at his funeral, and of course it was. Tray, the choir director at the church, let me know in advance that they were singing that anthem this morning. He didn't want me caught off guard. The choir is truly amazing every week, but when they sang this hymn today, I just felt Tom so near. I am grateful to Tray for letting me know, but I did want to be there for that. These kinds of things do not get any easier. Will they ever?

Monday, March 2, 2020

I seem to be in a routine. I go to work two mornings a week, do paperwork a third morning. Housework, yard work, taking care of two dogs during the day, dinner with Ben most nights. He likes to cook, so I am happy to let him.

Tuesday, March 3, 2020

Daddy died forty years ago today. He was a young fifty-eight, ten years younger than I am now. I recall it all so clearly. The call from Mom. Rushing to their house. Gladys and Clarence showing up.

Wendell was out of town, preaching at a Virginia church where he once served. He said that he drove into town, drove by my parents' home and saw the funeral signs. These were pre-cell phone days, so he had not been notified that a parishioner had died. We were in the middle of a major snowstorm covering the East Coast. Samp and I had driven his VW beetle as far into my younger sisters' neighborhood as we could and walked the rest of the way. We had to let them know, and both my sister and her husband were deaf so we could not call.

We had celebrated the day before as Terri and Larry were expecting their first child. She miscarried later, which we all contributed to the stress of losing Daddy.

Wendell conducted Daddy's service, and his words are still with me today.

Wednesday, March 4, 2020

Still going through books. I found a stack of old cookbooks that were boxed away. One was a cookbook that Donna and Carl had given to Mom for Mother's Day one year. When we moved her into assisted living, we kept some things. I had probably never even looked in this book, but as I picked it up, a paper fell out. This is what was written on it, in Mom's handwriting.

WIDOW'S WORDS

I think now as I lie here in the dark

Of all the things we meant to do.

Alone they are nothing.

But who wants to listen to the solo sung of widowhood?

No one but another widow, for she is the only one who knows the bitter truth.

It never gets better.

It only gets ordinary.

UNKNOWN

I believe that Mom was reaching out to me with these words.

Thursday, March 5, 2020

Things that I have learned this first year.

One thing that I have learned is that it is harder to come home to an empty house than it is to never leave.

I have learned that no one walks in these shoes, as I cannot walk in another's. Some friends have an insight into how to respond or how not to respond. How to listen, to share, to show caring, to encourage. Those are the people I need around me.

Keeping busy is key.

Enjoying the good memories and surrounding myself with his pictures, furniture he made, his writing and his sayings are the things that help me most.

Spending time with his son, our son, is a lifeline.

Friday, March 6, 2020

Had lunch with Anna Gray. That was fun. She had loved Tom and had been in our home for meals, chatting, and had been in church together. She loved the Blessing of the Animals service, which was one of Tom's favorites also.

Saturday, March 7, 2020

Tis the season for yard work, but it keeps me busy and tires me out.

Sunday, March 8, 2020

Today is Ben's thirtieth birthday. It is also Emily's birthday. Yes, they shared birthdays and had celebrated together since she was fourteen, so this was a difficult day.

We went to brunch together and he had some of his guy friends over at his apartment to eat pizza that evening. I know it is so hard. This is the problem with parenting as your child ages. When they are little, you can almost always fix the problem, but as they age, all you can do is listen, support and love. You can't fix it.

The grief surrounds us both.

This was my letter to him:

Dear Ben,

Your father did a lot of wonderful things, for me and for others, but the greatest was giving me you. I would never have imagined the depth of love that I feel for you and have felt since I first held you. I was scared and nervous that I would not be a good mother, that I would not know what to do, that I would not wake up to care for you during the night and numerous other fears. But we survived!

I made some mistakes as a mom and as a person, but through all of my bumbling, somehow you have grown into an exceptional person, filled with concern and empathy for our world and her people. Please continue to think, to care, to work towards helping this tired world.

We have such great memories of you growing up. Not just the Christmas mornings or birthday parties, trips or celebrations, but the daily happenings. Watching you hide Easter eggs with Aunt June, hiding her apples, fishing with your dad, our Christmas Eve a.m. cookies, reading nightly until I fell asleep, learning to ride a bike, Scouts, youth activities, soccer, school projects and yes, even band. All of those boxes of pictures do paint a story of a child who was so loved and such fun to be with.

Since June 2019, the relationship between us has changed. I have always felt extremely close to you and that we were able to talk and confide in each other about anything. But since June, the ability to share our open wounds, to cry, to laugh, to be pissed, to be honest, has been a literal lifesaver. Thank you for these past months of caring and keeping me afloat. I have repeatedly mentioned that Woody, Mac, Donna and Carl, along with numerous others, were our support, and they were. But you were mine. Thank you for that.

I have always said that I wanted you to be happy. My prayer for you has deepened. Yes, I do want your happiness, but I also want you to experience the love that I was fortunate enough to experience for your dad and for you. They are different loves, and both ones that if life is good to you, you will also have to treasure. There is nothing like it.

Through all the years ahead, never doubt that you were wanted, loved, respected and needed.

I love you,

Mom

Monday, March 9, 2020

I am in a parking garage connected to a department store and I cannot locate my car.

Those who know me would say, "What else is new?" Each floor of the department store is connected to a floor in the parking garage, so you have to reenter the store to go down or upstairs to reach the next level. So, I go up and down, around and around, three complete cycles. Finally, I sit down and call Ben to tell him that I know where I am but cannot find my car.

Then I wake up.

Well, I think. That dream was easy to interpret. I am looking for my late husband and/or I am looking for answers about this pandemic we are living.

Tuesday, March 10, 2020

What is this virus? How bad will it get? Where is my partner to talk things over with and help me make decisions? We were a team, a partnership. As he used to say when conducting a marriage: "no upper management."

Wednesday, March 11, 2020

There are closings around the country. Linda and I talk. John still working from home in Seattle.

Large cities seem to be the most affected at this point. Will people take this seriously?

Thursday, March 12, 2020

Had lunch again with Stuart and Susan. She is a retired nurse, but she had no answers about this pandemic either. Seems like this is totally new ground.

Friday, March 13, 2020

They are discussing closing schools. If so, perhaps we will be back up and running after spring break.

Saturday, March 14, 2020

I spent the day getting speech lessons together for my kids to take home on Monday, just in case they need them. Some of my students do not have access to internet nor do they have a laptop or tablet. Some do, but they share them. Seems like the best way is to send home a packet designed for each individual child and stay in touch with the parents by email. I'll make copies of everything Monday and put into packets to go home.

Sunday, March 15, 2020

No school tomorrow. Schools closed indefinitely. Wow, that happened fast. I'll go in anyway and get stuff finalized and figure out how to get it to the kids.

Monday, March 16, 2020

Went to MSA, and Tessa and I got speech packets together. Parents of the older kids coming by in the afternoon to get books and information from the classroom teachers. If they have siblings in speech therapy, we can send it that way. If not, the school will mail the packets home.

Very sad day.

This is a day that I needed to come home to my best friend.

Tuesday, March 17, 2020

A very close friend has a mother dying as I write these words. She lives less than thirty minutes away, the other side of Charleston, but I can't do anything but text or call or send prayers. I do recall how present she was to me both during Tom's illness and afterwards for the past five months. She would drop flowers from her yard off at my house or a note. Or send a text. I remember, and I want her to remember that I was there for her also.

Wednesday, March 18, 2020

The landscaping company came to sod. One of the few types of companies that can still work during this pandemic. Ben and I plan to try and do take-out once a week and tip generously so as to help the restaurants.

Thursday, March 19, 2020

Got a haircut this a.m. They are not closed, but who knows if that might happen.

Friday, March 20, 2020

I was invited to brunch at Donna and Carl's house.

Went to Mac's office and signed power of attorney papers so Ben has my power of attorney. I had not even thought of that, as Tom had mine and I had his. David (our CPA) suggested that to me, so I called Mac and he got it done.

Saturday, March 21, 2020

I was scheduled to attend a neighborhood dinner at the Shulers' house tonight. They cancelled due to the virus. Seems smart to me.

Sunday, March 22, 2020

Grief is with one constantly. Not daily or occasionally or sometimes. It is the one constant in my day. I cry every day. Not sobbing, not for long periods, but daily. I never know when it is coming, but I know that it will. It used to be that church was the hardest thing for me to attend.

We were married at The French Huguenot Church thirty-three years ago, my husband became one of the ministers there after his retirement from the university, and they became our church family. Our son and our niece were married there also, so it was filled with memories. Walking in the door, sitting in the pew, his lack of presence on the platform was all overwhelming. I made myself continue to go, as I wanted and needed to be there, but it was so hard. This had gradually gotten easier, but now none of us can attend due to COVID-19.

Monday, March 23, 2020

Grief during a pandemic. I told my older sister one day that I felt guilty thinking about myself and my grief when the world was literally turned upside down. She responded that I was dealing with two major things at the same time and I should not feel guilty. But guilt is there.

Tuesday, March 24, 2020

When this COVID-19 hit our world, I, like so many others, went searching for answers, for comfort, for advice. For more than forty of my sixty-eight years, his had been the voice that I listened to, that I turned to for assurance, for advice, for discussion. I kept thinking, "What would Wendell do? What would he say?" I longed for his words. Then one morning, during my daily cleaning out, organizing, etc., of our study stuff and attic stuff, I happened upon a box that I thought was tax papers. It wasn't, but it was a fun box of memories. Cards from Ben to me on occasions like birthdays and Mother's Day, certificates from his academic achievements in middle school, programs, etc. Even some old pictures. In the middle of that was a sermon entitled "For the Living of these days." Now keep in mind that all sermons are labeled, in a file folder, in a drawer in a file cabinet (well several drawers). This one was not in a folder. It was just there, in that box, on that morning when I needed it. And yes, the sermon was timely, and spoke to me, and helped me, even though it was written in 1998.

Wednesday, March 25, 2020

Friends have commented to me that this quarantine must be harder on me than most as I am totally alone. Actually, in many ways, I think it is easier on me. Ben comes every night after work and cooks dinner. We talk and he stays until about eight, and then Barkley and I go to bed.

I fill the morning hours with housework or yard work or books and organizing work. I read. I walk Barkley. I don't have the desire to be out in restaurants or stores. Many many people have things much worse than I do. I have a home, heat or AC, food and a son who cares for me.

Yes, I am one of the lucky ones.

Thursday, March 26, 2020

456 cases
9 deaths

Governor McMaster says a statewide work or stay-home order is unnecessary because people are voluntarily complying with his earlier orders and requests to avoid gatherings and avoid social distancing.

Friday, March 27, 2020

It's becoming more difficult to even know what day it is. Everyday so much the same.

Saturday, March 28, 2020

660 cases

15 deaths

Hundreds flock to Folly Beach after the attorney general says only the governor can shut down cities. City council meets that evening and votes to re-close anyway after consulting with attorneys.

Schools ordered closed through April.

Sunday, March 29, 2020

One thing that I have realized about Wendell's time of death is that I am relieved that he did not have to endure this pandemic. With his lung issues, he would have been such high risk. We would not have dared for Ben to enter the house, or for me to leave it. If he could have been well, I would have preferred to go through this with him, but with him sick…no.

Monday, March 30, 2020

I would never have imagined such a time as this. People are handling the "restrictions" so differently. Some in denial. Some in fear. Ben wears a mask in public, but says at least half of people do not.

Tuesday, March 31, 2020

1,083 cases
22 deaths

Non-essential businesses closed.

Mount Pleasant, Charleston and Columbia declare work or home order.

Wednesday, April 1, 2020

So, my good friend Sylvia and I decided to have a girls' evening during the pandemic with all precautions taken. She picked up a spinach salad and came to my house. Sitting in the living room, drinking a KY mule in the copper mugs, she suddenly said, "Your shirt is wet and it looks just like a heart!" It did. I just smiled. It was Tom's way of saying he was glad I was with my friend. I believe that.

Thursday, April 2, 2020

Received this from one of his former students. The lives that Tom touched were so many. Heather flew from Vermont to Charleston when he was in the hospital, even though she knew it had to be a short visit, in order to see him one more time.

> I recently returned to my old church via online. The minister, Elissa, delivers profound and challenging messages. As I listen to them, I am reminded of Dr. Guerry's sermons. I told her that her sermons made me think of him and she wants to hear more about him. I look forward to sharing more about the powerful impact he made and sharing his sermons. There was also a sermon that she gave that talked about the people in our lives who believed in us and encouraged us. Dr. Guerry was one of those people for me and his words of encouragement and affirmation still remain with me. He was a special man. My thoughts are with you and Ben as you continue on your journey of loss.

Friday, April 3, 2020

Ben and I took a bin full of old albums and a couple of boxes of books to a bookstore in North Charleston that buys them. Very nice man met us in the back, masked. Ben placed the bins and the boxes into their storage room and he said they will let them sit for five to seven days before checking to see if they want them. We are living in strange times.

Saturday, April 4, 2020

Today was supposed to be a family wedding downtown at Circular Congregation. One of Tom's cousins' daughter was getting married, or supposed to. The wedding was postponed as so many are these days.

Sunday, April 5, 2020

Gracious Lord,

We do not know what tomorrow may bring, yet we do not fear for our confidence is in you whose ways are good and whose heart is kind.

Because we believe that you are the God of comfort, we seek your peace.

Because we believe that you are the God of wisdom we seek your guidance.

Because we believe that you are the God of love, we seek your presence.

In the name of Jesus.

Amen

One of my husband's prayers.

Monday, April 6, 2020

2,332 cases

48 deaths

These are SC stats. Governor now issued a mandatory home/work order as people not complying to the voluntary orders.

Tuesday, April 7, 2020

The days do seem to drag on. Palm Sunday has passed with no church services except online. Grateful for our church staff and so many other ministers for posting services.

Wednesday, April 8, 2020

Still getting small signals, hard to define exactly if they are that unique, but I continue to look at the clock and it is 9:20…his birthday. I smile and talk to him, so I'm going to just pretend he is here. I need him to be.

Thursday, April 9, 2020

Maundy Thursday. My first exposure to a Maundy Thursday service was one that my husband led. Families sitting around tables. Scripture. Communion.

Now everything is turmoil.

Friday, April 10, 2020

The Tenebrae Service at our former church was one of my favorites. It was so quiet, and meaningful. Every year as we sat in darkness, even though I knew it was coming, I jumped when the Bible was slammed shut, to indicate the closing of the cave.

Saturday, April 11, 2020

We had fun at Easter at our house. Every year I videotaped Wendell and Ben dying eggs. Kind of the same thing annually, except Ben kept growing. I have enjoyed watching those old videos.

Sunday, April 12, 2020

I'm angry today. It is Easter and I really don't care. All of my life Easter has been special. From the three sisters wearing yellow Easter dresses every year because yellow was Daddy's favorite color, to becoming a Christian and following the story. As my faith grew and I began to understand Lent, Maundy Thursday, Good Friday (thanks, Scott McBroom) and Easter morning, Easter became more important. Living with a minister did not diminish that at all. In fact it enhanced it. But today, I don't want to think about it. I don't want Easter without Wendell. I don't want Easter with this pandemic we are living through (or not). I'm angry. And I am angry at myself because my problems are so few. I have so much, when so many do not. People are dying, people are afraid, people are lonely and scared. I need to shut up and think about others.

Monday, April 13, 2020

3,439 cases
87 deaths

Tuesday, April 14, 2020

Thinking about Amy today. After her Dad died, she asked me to give her a couple of his shirts and 12 of his ties. She took those items and created a unique pillow that stays on my bed. It even has the buttons from the shirt down the back of the pillow and the ties were used to make a bow. She has to be the most creative person that I know. What a special gift and one that is so him!

Wednesday, April 15, 2020

Amy and John's twenty-fifth wedding anniversary.

Thursday, April 16, 2020

Isn't it funny (not really) how life goes on. My world stopped and everyone keeps on with their jobs, their vacations, their shopping, their lives. We have an international pandemic, yet we still go to the store, get gas, work at jobs from home, cook, pay bills. Are we robots?

Friday, April 17, 2020

"These days cry out, as never before, for us to pay attention, so we can move through them and get our joy and pride back." Anne Lamott

Saturday, April 18, 2020

I believe that each individual has the right to grieve, and to grieve in their own way. No one truly can comprehend the multitude of feelings. No one can truly share them. But without my two sisters and their husbands, my nieces, my step-daughter, my minister friend, my lawyer friend, my close friends and most especially, my son, I would not have been upright to sit and type these words.

They are all a gift to me and one that I don't take for granted.

Sunday, April 19, 2020

Have begun to listen to our services online every Sunday and I am so grateful for our ministers , music director, choir, laypersons, for making this happen. It's very comforting when we cannot attend in person.

I also occasionally watch church on YouTube. A former minister and his wife are leading a church in Canada that I watch, and another minster friend is in Asheville and their service is on FB.

Monday, April 20, 2020

The days continue in a blur. Except for my morning walk with Barkley when I occasionally see neighbors out and Ben's daily pop-in, I see no one. This virus is much more than anyone could have ever imagined.

Tuesday, April 21, 2020

Ben and I head downtown to the church cemetery for the stone placement. No one is there except us and the guy from the monument company. A kind, competent man. He had some trouble as the urn was not placed deep enough due to Charleston brick which is all over the city. He worked on that and got everything done. He is definitely an expert. Grateful for the way that he handled everything. During the hour or so that we were there, Ben and I quietly walked around the cemetery and reflected. It was a holy time for both of us.

Wednesday, April 22, 2020

I experienced an interesting interaction today at the grocery store. An elderly lady was checking out in front of me. Of course, all of us were masked and socially distanced, but even after her groceries were checked out, she did not move up to pay. We all waited as she went slowly though her wallet. Finally, she said to the cashier to cancel her groceries, that she could not find her credit card. I offered to pay her $11. 61 bill, and she refused. I offered several times and she said she couldn't let me do it. Finally, the cashier kindly said, "she wants to, let her". The customer asked for my information so she could pay me back and I told her no, that I would someday need help as well and that we all needed to be kind. The situation left me with some unsettling thoughts. I didn't feel good that I had helped someone, I didn't feel grateful that I had the means to help someone, I felt alone. The realization that my entire world has been shaken. That from October 19, 2019 on, I face this future. No partner. No one to share life's ups and downs, frustrations, delights or joys. It hit me hard.

Thursday, April 23, 2020

In every person's life there are certain defining moments. Some are memorable in a good way while others are not so good. Some are of our own choosing; some are beyond our control. Decisions made to begin, decisions made to end. Decisions that will alter the course of the rest of our lives.

Words taken from Tom's last sermon, June 23, 2019

Friday, April 24, 2020

Today is Caison's twenty-first birthday. Wendell's first grandson. He loved that young man and was so proud of him.

Saturday, April 25, 2020

Today is June's birthday.

Sunday, April 26, 2020

As Barkley and I sit vigil at almost 3 am, I can't help but remember so many couples that Wendell Guerry conducted weddings for and the happy memories that we share. Death is hard, and lonely. Tonight, I grow increasingly thankful for our memories, for the road we have traveled, for the amazing gift of our son, Ben Guerry, and for the friends and family walking this final journey with us.

I wrote this October 16, 2019.

Monday, April 27, 2020

Today we celebrated the life of one of the most amazing men that I've ever known, Reverend Doctor Wendell Thomas Guerry. He was a neighbor that became a friend, and then became family. Throughout my life, he has given me many joys and countless things to be thankful for. Of those things, he has given me a best friend that I call a brother, an unending welcome into his home, and the blessing of my marriage. When I first asked Mr. Tom to marry JD and I, he told me of a memory he had of standing in his kitchen, looking through the window above the sink and watching me play in his back yard. He said that he knew then how fearless, passionate and strong-willed I would be when I got older. Mr. Tom gave JD and I words of advice as we began planning the intimate details of our wedding. A plan that Mr. Tom was deeply intertwined in. His presence was a comfort to me for more than one reason but after today, I think I can narrow it down to one. He was the one that has been fearless, passionate and strong-willed all along. He fought endlessly to stand beside us on one of the most important days of our lives and join us in union for life. His love and kindness toward me will never be forgotten and I will live with that same intention for those in my life. All of my love is with you today, Vickie Monroe Guerry and Ben Guerry just like every day.

Written by Betsy Wallace Crance, October 23, 2019.

Tuesday, April 28, 2020

I have learned that no one walks in these shoes, as I cannot walk in another's. Some friends have an insight into how to respond, or how not to respond. How to listen, to share, to show caring, to encourage. Those are the people I need around me.

Wednesday, April 29, 2020

"Perfect happiness is a beautiful sunset, the giggle of a grandchild, the first snowfall. It's the little things that make happy moments, not the grand events. Joy comes in sips, not gulps." Sharon Draper

Thursday, April 30, 2020

6,095 cases
244 deaths

In Charleston, city parks prepare to open.

Friday, May 1, 2020

Looks like school graduations will look very different this year. Some people being very creative, following guidelines to give the graduates a safe taste of celebrations.

Saturday, May 2, 2020

Recently, a friend used the phrase "God's wonderful movements." He went on to explain that he was convinced that we are in each other's paths for specific times and purposes. What an amazing, supportive statement! Tom and I believe that too. This church has been in our path and a part of our journey for many years. We were married here in 1986. We became members and a part of this church family in 2011 and since that time have grown to love this place. The sense of worship, the incredible music and most of all, you, the people. We have laughed and cried together, shared holy moments and some not so holy. We have been through the highs and lows of life and have supported and cared for each other during those times. Thank you for allowing us to minister with you and to share your journeys.

Words spoken by me, June 23, 2019, at The French Huguenot Church.

Sunday, May 3, 2020

Today was the date for our annual neighborhood picnic. It is a time to relax with neighbors and eat barbeque and elect officers. Cancelled.

Monday, May 4, 2020

"My friend is that one whom I can associate with my choicest thought." Thoreau

Tuesday, May 5, 2020

"Whenever a crisis comes, an opportunity is created." I read these words while going through old papers from my late husband's files. They spoke to me as his words so often did. He did not mean an opportunity to make money, an opportunity to get ahead, an opportunity to think of self. I believe he meant an opportunity for doing something that can help the world. There is so much we can do from the safety of our homes.

We can donate to causes that benefit those struggling during these days.

We can call, email, text someone to let them know we are thinking of them and to check on their needs.

We can support our local restaurants who have take-out/pick-up services and leave a larger than normal tip.

We can keep our distance from persons having to work in grocery stores and other places, to respect their health.

We can stay home if we don't have to get out.

We can find a way to express our appreciation for the doctors and nurses and health-care providers who are frontline every day.

We can enjoy the beautiful season that we are in by walking and biking in our neighborhoods or by sitting outside in the sun.

We can listen to the scientists, and to those whose voices are filled with compassion and concern for people.

We can study and read and remember when it is time to vote.

We can read and self-reflect on what is truly important in our lives.

We can pray, not just for the people that we know and love, but for all of the people in the world. We keep reading, "We are in this together," and that doesn't mean just our country. This is true in this present situation that we face as a community, as a nation and as a world.

We can bring a smile to a face, and bring hope to those who need it.

I close with more of Tom's words:

We lay before you, O Lord, the deepest burdens of our hearts. Some of us have loved ones who languish in pain and illness. We place our trust in you for their healing. Some carry secret anxieties but they are not hidden from you. We seek release. Some have come here seeking a word of hope, a reason to hope, looking for a way beyond despair. Speak that word to them, we pray.

Amen

Wednesday, May 6, 2020

6,936 cases
305 deaths

Thursday, May 7, 2020

How do people go on when their life partner is gone? Why do you want to go on? If I could do my life over again, I would start from the first time we made love. Oh, I would make a couple of big changes, a couple of different decisions, but the end result would always be becoming his wife. I never felt we were in anything but a partnership. We both gave and we both took. We solved problems together, we supported each other and loved each other. We also had fights and said words that were painful.

Nothing can be changed. The rest of my life I will wonder if I will ever see him again. If we will ever be together again.

Why is this so hard?

Friday, May 8, 2020

The neighborhood put out luminary bags at dusk in memory of folks who had cancer. It was pretty but not the effect hoped for as the houses are too far apart. Some people placed more than one bag. It was a nice, together thought.

Saturday, May 9, 2020

"Death leaves a heartache no one can heal, love leaves a memory no one can steal." From an Irish headstone

Sunday, May 10, 2020

Mother's Day.

There was a time in my life when I dreaded Mother's Day. I wanted so fiercely to be pregnant and to have a baby, but it was just not working out. My sisters and my friends were moms, and it was a difficult time. Then one Mother's Day, I went unhappily to church, and I heard a sermon from a very wise minister talking about the value of womanhood, indeed personhood. The sermon was on Hannah and her difficulties in getting pregnant. From that sermon, and from personal reflections, I have concluded that one does not have to give birth to be a mother. A mother loves unconditionally, supports you, cries with and for you, laughs with you and listens to you. How many people male and female in today's world fit the role of "mother," but who have never given birth? I think of those with aging parents, where the roles have reversed, of aunts who have been the role models for young girls, of teachers, of ministers, of men who for various reasons serve as exceptional "moms," of those who are moms to our beloved pets, and on and on. So, this Mother's Day weekend, I give thanks to ALL those who are mothers. You make our world a better place.

I wrote this in 2015, and it still rings true to me today. Yesterday, in going through some files, I came across the above-mentioned sermon. Included in Tom's words were these, "Motherhood is great, Womanhood is even greater, but Personhood is the best." If only in today's world, all personhood could be respected and celebrated.

Monday, May 11, 2020

I made the hard decision not to go back to Meeting Street Academy next year. I wanted to work another year. I love my job, the money would help, and the desire to feel purposeful is critical.

Having worked as a speech pathologist for forty-five years and having loved my job, I felt that I needed to not end another part of who I am. I had lost so much of me when Tom died.

However, this virus had another plan.

I called Dirk and we talked. He was understanding of course. My age, the population that I work with, and Ben not needing to suffer another loss if possible, were all factors in the decision.

So, I grieve, yet am grateful for the end of an amazing career that was a part of who I am.

Husband gone, career gone. Wow…

Tuesday, May 12, 2020

For Wendell's 80th birthday, I decided to make him a book about his life in ministry. I spent a lot of time on this book, contacting persons from his past, parishioners and former students, couples that he had married, staff from former churches that he served, seminary friends and colleagues. Amy, Ben and I wrote in it as well. I collected pictures of churches and couples and baptisms and anything else that I could think of. I gave it to him in February as I was excited and could not wait for his September birthday. I am so very glad that I did, as he died 27 days after his 80th birthday. He seemed to enjoy looking at this book and reading what folks had written, and he even took it to the hospital with him.

Below is a part of what I wrote to him:

> I was not there the day of your ordination, nor did I experience seminary with you. I did not share the first years of your ministry. You came into my life as my parent's pastor, and later on, mine. The care that you provided our family when Daddy died, and your words of comfort and healing for both Mom and Dad's services will forever be with me. Our common bond of church and ministry with the deaf created a friendship, and later a love.
>
> We have traveled roads together from Round O to Black Creek, Allendale, Sycamore, Kline, Ulmer,

Pompion Hill and Strawberry Chapel, and finally resting on Church Street. What memories, what gracious folks, what memorable meals over tables in homes and fellowship halls.

Thank you for sharing that with me.

Throughout it all, you have remained the best minister that I have ever heard speak. From the beginning, your sermons spoke to me, taught me, made me think. I have grown theologically and politically because of you and have been exposed to life experiences that have forever changed the little innocent girl that you once knew.

Thank you for the past 32 years. You really are the "wind beneath my wings", and I hope that in some small ways, I have been a slight breeze beneath yours.

Wednesday, May 13, 2020

The desire of his touch is an actual pain. I look at pictures where we are standing close together, and I can almost feel his body beside mine. You can't say things like this to people. You think them, you feel them, you acknowledge them. The pain is real.

Thursday, May 14, 2020

Life during a pandemic. We all seem to move a bit slower, as there is more time to do things. Many activities have been totally stopped, and many others we are continuing to explore new ways to accomplish.

Woody sends an online devotion every morning. Reflection seems to be a good way to start the day.

I think of the years that Wendell and I rushed through the days. Care for our child, work, house and yard work, church work and volunteer work. Always busy. Always on the run. If we had known, if we had made time for each other more. If he were here (in good health of course) sharing these quieter days with me. Oh, what I would give for that.

Friday, May 15, 2020

8,407 cases
380 deaths

Today is my niece Kate's birthday. She is a flight attendant and risks her life every day that she works. She is taking all precautions, but is it enough? I pray so.

Saturday, May 16, 2020

Days seem to run together. Not working, no church services in person, no real social activities…life is very strange. My mind can't seem to separate it all. Grief, anger, virus, loss, sadness, alone time, fear, gratitude.

Sunday, May 17, 2020

Another Sunday comes around. All of the days are so very different, for all of us. People weary of masking, of staying home, of social distancing. Amazing how new vocabulary has popped up.

Social distancing

6 feet apart

COVID

Masking

Monday, May 18, 2020

I got this email from a friend, Mary. It made me laugh. We need humor in our world right now and I need humor in my life as well. I remember watching Wendell laugh until he cried watching movies such as Monty Python and the Holy Grail. I didn't share his type of humor, but I laughed with him as his delight made me laugh.

> Heard a Dr. on TV saying in this time of Coronavirus staying at home we should focus on inner peace. To achieve this we should always finish things we start and we all could use more calm in our lives. I looked through my house to find things i'd started and hadn't finished, so I finished off a bottle of Merlot, a bottle of Chardonnay, a bodle of Baileys, a butle of wum, tha mainder of Valiumun srciptuns, an a box a chocletz. Yu haf no idr how feckin fablus I feel rite now. Sned this to all who need inner piss. An telum u luvum. And two hash yer wands, stafe
>
> day avrybobby!!!

Tuesday, May 19, 2020

Another book given to me by a friend is *Miracle on 31ˢᵗ Street* by Susan Sparks. "Christmas Cheer Every Day of the Year, Grinch to Gratitude in 26 days!"

It's not about death or about grief, but it is about hope and cheer. I read a chapter every night. Thank you, Mitch!

Wednesday, May 20, 2020

9,175 cases
407 deaths in SC

A national poll finds strong fear among Americans about a new wave of infections spreading as states loosen restrictions and continue reopening. Memorial Day weekend looms.

Thursday, May 21, 2020

Our country needs leadership as we did during other tragic events and times. America is devoid of that kind of leadership right now. It weighs heavily.

Friday, May 22, 2020

Ben and I drove to Meeting Street Academy and boxed up the materials that I am taking with me and boxed up all other materials—mine as well as the school's materials that are staying. I plan to send my kept items to Kate Bouser, a young, smart SLP in Philly that I have known her entire life. I am so proud of her career track, as well as proud of the person that she is.

I am keeping some of my therapy books, as I hope someday to read to a grandchild! Some were Ben's books when he was growing up that I have used in therapy for years.

It feels strange. There is a finality to it all.

Saturday, May 23, 2020

I have found cards that Tom gave me through the years. With his humor there were always inserted comments from him, but I read them over and over. I have a pile of them in my bedroom where they are accessible to me when I just need them. A reassurance of his love?

Below is one of Wendell's poems. He loved to write poetry and started writing poems when he was young.

I do plan to compile all of them and have them bound for Ben and Amy to have to keep.

That's going to be a job, but not as much as getting all those sermons together and bound.

Good to have projects.

SPO-DEE-0-DEE

You cause the grass to grow for the cattle, and plants for people to use, to bring forth food from the earth, and wine to gladden the human heart. **Psalm 104:14-15 (NRSV)**

Some pious folks think
That no Christian should drink,
And when offered some wine
Should politely decline,
And must always eschew
What's immoral to do
(We must let our little lights shine.)

Their argument runs
That the godliest ones
Always turn up their noses

At rum or Four Roses.
The righteous refuse
Every version of booze
(Except secretly, one supposes.)

They say with their bias
It's clearly impious
To go round describing
The Savior imbibing
Or making the potion –
A scurrilous notion!
(To which one should not be subscribing.)

But are they forgetting
The wine at the wedding
In gallon aplenty
For serving the many?
Did Jesus produce
Nothing stronger than juice?
(If so, who would want to drink any?)

Since drinking is risky
One might avoid whiskey
And try to stay clear
Of an excess of beer
Though moderate wine
Is quite biblically fine.
(The kind of thing we like to hear.)

©2012 by Wendell Thomas Guerry

Monday, May 25, 2020

Today in Minnesota, an African American, George Floyd, was killed by a police officer. The video shows the policeman kneeling on the man's neck for more than eight minutes. Such a inexcusable tragedy. When will this killing stop?

Tuesday, May 26, 2020

Protests in Minnesota and other cities across America. This senseless killing has to stop. Until we can look at each other as brothers and sisters, how can we ever relate, unite, understand, listen and learn.

Wednesday, May 27, 2020

10,623 cases
466 deaths
New daily record in SC

Thursday, May 28, 2020

The world has gone crazy. It is like a movie, except it doesn't end. Where are our leaders?

Isn't it enough for people like me to try and deal with the death of a loved one? Now we have a virus, terrible racial inequalities, anger everywhere, a leader who doesn't know how to lead—but to incite. Our world needs the best leaders right now. We need FDR, Churchill, Lincoln. We need leaders with the morals of Jimmy Carter and the brains of Clinton and Obama.

Friday, May 29, 2020

Masses gathered for Memorial Day celebrations. People are tired of staying in. Pictures show crowded beaches, with no masks nor social distancing. I have a feeling that this is not going to turn out well.

I recently read this:

> Fear is the path to the Dark Side. Fear leads to anger, anger leads to hate, hate leads to suffering. Yoda

> I enjoyed Star Wars, but as I read these words they seemed to speak differently to me. I hold a lot of fear these days, as well as a lot of anger. I don't hate though and I am grateful for that.

Sunday, May 31, 2020

Our ministers have an even heavier task of reaching their congregations. Lack of face-to-face ministry, a pandemic, racial inequalities rising to the forefront, scared and lonely people. I wish Tom was here.

An email from a former student:

> I've been thinking about a single class period with Dr. Guerry that changed my outlook on the world and my faith in profound ways.

> People's memories of him and his influence continue coming.

Tuesday, June 2, 2020

The protests continue around the nation, and indeed around the world. People are rising up to protest the 400-plus years of systemic racism. People of all ages, colors, nationalities are begging for their voices to be heard. The protests are mainly peaceful and it appears most marchers are wearing masks.

Wednesday, June 3, 2020

The protests appear to have taken the headlines away from the virus.

Thursday, June 4, 2020

"Strength grows in the moments when you think you can't go on but you keep going anyway." Anonymous

Because of Wendell's death the county has decided that I no longer qualify for the 4 percent property tax. I have to complete forms and submit by a deadline, or my house payment will significantly increase. Wow, I don't think this paperwork will ever end.

Saturday, June 6, 2020

Not sure if it is just me, or if everything has slowed down. No alarms to get up, no rush for completing tasks. It would be easy to sit down and read and nap and not do anything, but I recognize how bad that would be. I try to do one thing to the yard daily and one thing to the house. Then I write, take care of the dogs' needs, eat, read, nap and wait for Ben to come by for Rascal and/or dinner. An entirely different pace from last year. This time a year ago, Ben had just gotten the declaration from Emily, Tom was with us but going in the wrong direction, and I was still working.

Sunday, June 7, 2020

Donna and Carl left for Holden Beach. They have been doing this with Carl's family for a long time and they have thirty family members meeting this year! They discussed it at length but are taking every precaution. I pray they have fun and stay well.

Monday, June 8, 2020

Paperwork day. State Farm. Tax stuff. I don't like adulting alone.

Tuesday, June 9, 2020

Busy social day. Louise came over for brunch. No hugging, social distancing. It was wonderful to sit and chat. She graciously looked all through Tom's project book that he had made a few years ago with most of the creations that he had made. It was fun sharing that with her.

Elise came for happy hour. She has the care of her eighty-plus-year-old dad, her brother has stage 4 cancer, there are problems with one of her daughters, so happy hour is a way for her to talk, and it helps me to be the listener.

This world is a mess and being kind and reaching out is something all of us can do.

Wednesday, June 10, 2020

Officially closed my private practice today. It is another strange finality.

Thursday, June 11, 2020

Ben bought a boat! It is something he can do that is social, but safe. He needs this, I think. Some folks might say he should be saving that money for a house or a rainy day, but at this time in his life, with his current situation, I think the boat is a great thing. He lives in Charleston after all!

Friday, June 12, 2020

I was born in the mountains of West Virginia and grew up in the mountains of North Carolina. I did my undergraduate degree in the hills of Boone. Mountains are in my blood. They are a calming place, a sacred place, a place that provides strength and comfort to me like no other place can. I so need to be in the mountains. I need to sit and look at the mountains in silence, to reflect, to shed tears, to gain some kind of ability to keep on moving and living. I fear I am losing that here in the Lowcountry. I love this place, it is home. It is beautiful. But it is not my mountains.

Saturday, June 13, 2020

Kristin and Woody came over for dinner tonight. First time we have tried that during the pandemic. They have been quarantining also and it seemed safe enough. No hugs, kept apart from each other. Ben makes some good shrimp and grits!

Sunday, June 14, 2020

Donna and Carl back after a week at Holden Beach. They are self-quarantining for two weeks. Such strange times.

Monday, June 15, 2020

I have realized that Wendell was my hero. In addition to being my love, my best friend, the father of my child, he was my hero. These days cry out to me with a great need to listen to his advice, his words, his strength.

Tuesday, June 16, 2020

Twenty-six years ago, today, we moved into this house. It was raining and as I stood in our bedroom and looked out at the treetops, I felt I was in a tree house. That feeling remains to this day. This was our third house as a couple, and by far our favorite. Ben was four years old when we moved here. It has been an amazing twenty-six years, filled with laughter, friends, food, projects, TIME.

Wednesday, June 17, 2020

Five years ago, today, a white supremacist walked into Mother Emmanuel Church and killed nine innocent persons. We remember, and as the protests grow in our city and in others, we promise once again to do better, to love more, to be kind, to listen, to work together, to reach out. God give us both the strength and the willingness to follow through. Four hundred-plus years is way too long.

My husband's words, written for the anniversary of the Mother Emanuel Church slayings.

> Lord, as we consider and remember tragedy that has fallen upon people of our city, our nation, and our world, we confess that we are confused and troubled and fearful.
> Yet, we do not lose heart, for our confidence is in you.
> Because we believe that you are the God of comfort, we seek your presence for those who grieve in every land.
> Because we believe that you are the God of wisdom, we seek your guidance for those who govern in every land.
> Because we believe that you are the God of peace, we seek your deliverance from hatred and violence in every land.
> Because we believe that you are the God of love, we lift our heavy hearts to you.
> Hear our silent prayers.

Thursday, June 18, 2020

I am supposed to be in Wilmington right now. I was to have gone to Linda and John's house yesterday and stayed a couple of nights. However due to the virus and her children's concerns, we cancelled the trip. It's ok. I understand and it probably was smart. But it would have been fun.

Friday, June 19, 2020

A friend and church member texted me and said, "I sure wish we had Tom here to guide us." That's how I feel too. I miss his guidance and his support, his love and his words, every day, in so many ways. I know every love is different. I understand that my feelings are just that, my feelings. But does everyone who has lost a spouse feel this complete void in their existence? I have always been independent, had my own career, my own interests, my own life. But I am seeing how intertwined they were. From that first kiss, I belonged to him and he belonged to me. There were times when I doubted that, when I believed it was over and that we couldn't survive together, but we did. We managed to grab ahold of each other and to ride out the storms. Gosh, what I would give to do it all again.

"When the world seems too much with us, when we get so caught up in ourselves, so distressed over our problems, so weighed down with our troubles, maybe what we need most to hear is not that Jesus is coming to take us out of this vale of tears, but that he is with us now to carry us through it." WTG 7/22/18

Sunday, June 21, 2020

Father's Day. Ben and Amy's first Father's Day without their Dad. I know it has been hard on both of them.

I got Ben some parmesan crisps and a note from Rascal.

Amy and I texted a good bit and we hope to get lunch soon.

It was not supposed to be this hard on me, but it was. I was alone basically all day except for the dogs. Ben had to work and had plans that evening, which I encourage.

Louise called and I got in a good cry, with a friend who listens. As I told her, I'm not getting any better.

Monday, June 22, 2020

My sixty-ninth birthday. I was hoping for a better day than yesterday, as I know Ben has worked to make it a good day.

The day started with my first boat ride on his new boat. We toured the Charleston Harbor, up Hobcaw Creek, and up the Wando River. Saw the place where Tom baptized Ben in the living waters of the Wando, many years ago. Breezy, fun trip. Great start to the day.

Donna and Annie, Max and Finn came by and visited on the front porch. They wouldn't come in as they are still under quarantine from a week in a beach house with thirty of Carl's family. Max and Finn sang Happy Birthday to me. So cute and funny! They made me posters and brought me flowers from their gardens.

Brenda and Steve sent me a bouquet of beautiful flowers from Southern Pines. The note accompanying the flowers meant even more. "We know this will be a difficult birthday since it is the first since you lost your heart…"

Ben cooked steaks and mac and cheese and we had a great dinner and watched a movie.

Got through another first, with a lot of help from Ben, family and friends.

Tuesday, June 23, 2020

Amy and her boys came over and brought lunch. It was great to see them as we had not seen them since before the virus hit. No hugs of course, but a lot of laughter, a few tears and lots of memories.

Learned today of a young man who grew up in our neighborhood who was shot and killed last night. The bad stuff just keeps on happening.

Wednesday, June 24, 2020

One year ago, yesterday, was Tom's last sermon. After fifty-six years in ministry, he had to retire. The behind-the-scenes activity necessary to make this service possible involved amazing people. Friends in the church provided a bar stool with a back so he could sit. We took his oxygen. Phil asked Woody, a minister and longtime friend of our family, to read the liturgy. Special friends were invited. The choir sang Tom's favorite hymns and anthems. The Women of the Church presented him with a framed picture of the church. Ben read scripture. I did announcements. Where he managed to get the strength to get through the sermon I will never know. I stayed on the platform with him, per his request. He sat during the entire service except for the sermon where he got up, made it to the pulpit and then sat on the bar stool. The amazing strength, determination and yes stubbornness that it took for him to get through this surprised us all. But he did it. The church gave him a lovely reception afterwards. They fixed him a Bloody Mary and had lots of food, including a special bowl of Moon Pies. They knew that man!

Thursday, June 25, 2020

THE TIMES OF OUR LIVES

Ecclesiastes 3   *Romans 5:1-6.*

There is a popular axiom that extols the wisdom of quitting while you're ahead. Neither the word quitting nor fun adequately describes what Vickie and I are feeling. It would be hard to imagine a more fulfilling venture than we have had for the past eight years here among the Huguenots.

Please understand that we are not riding off into the sunset. As long as strength will allow, most Sundays will find us occupying a pew. Not every week, mind you, for one thing we've learned from you is that it's OK to lay out of church on occasion. Granted, some of you tend to overdo it but you need to know that retired preachers are allowed the most free cuts.

In every person's life there are certain defining moments. Some are memorable in a good way while others are not so good. Some are of our own choosing; some are beyond our control. Decisions made to begin, decisions made to end. Decisions that will alter the course of the rest of our lives.

There are times that are unique and unrepeatable. There are times where opportunities recur with great frequency.

June 23, 1963, 56 years ago today, was one such time in my life. On that Sunday afternoon I knelt and took my vows of ordination, committing my life to the service of God as a Christian minister, not knowing what to expect.

When I retired from CSU 11 years ago I had no idea of moving into a new place of ministry. But an opportunity fell into my lap so to speak and Vickie and I are so glad that it did. For it brought us to you.

Through all the years of my life I've been blessed beyond measure. In no sense has that been because of any special virtue on my part but the unearned opportunities that have turned me this way or that.

We understand what is meant when the referee calls a time out - or when a mother puts a recalcitrant child in time out. It's a bit like pressing the pause button. It's like the 23rd Psalm: "He makes me lie down...He restores my soul." Its purpose is renewal.

But if we're told, "You're out of time," that means it's over.

Trust God, see all, nor be afraid. Robert Browning, Rabbi Ben Ezra

The ancient Greeks, in whose language our New Testament was written, knew two different words each meaning time. The one, chronos, referred to quantitative time, time that can be measured, as days, weeks, years. The other is qualitative time, the time of opportunity.

The writer of Ecclesiastes understood the difference. He understood how our life moves. He talks about how what goes around comes around. There's nothing new under the sun, he says.

Time does its inexorable work, Slowing the step, dulling the ear, dimming the eye.

The song by Barbra Streisand asks the question have I stayed too long at the fair? And as though answering that question the Carpenters song says knowing when to leave may be the smartest thing that anyone can learn.

In one of his speeches President Kennedy referred to the oft quoted observation that the Chinese word for crisis is composed of two characters. One representing danger and the other representing opportunity.

Vickie has been and is the wind beneath my wings. Ben has been more than a son but a strong right arm as well. And to all three of us you have been a loving and caring family of faith.

One of the greatest of all social blunders is to overstay one's welcome. I would be grieved if that should apply to us.

When our Huguenot ancestors came to these shores in the 17th century they did not come on holiday. They did not come with any guarantees of safety or success or even survival. What they came with was an abiding trust in Almighty God. We have much to learn from them.

None of us knows what tomorrow may bring, or next year, or the next. A question that is often asked on job interviews is where do you see yourself in 10 years from now? But who can answer that with any certainty?

Once to every man and nation comes the moment to decide says the poet.

All shall be well.

AMEN

Wendell Thomas Guerry
The French Huguenot Church, Charleston, SC
June 23, 2019

Friday, June 26, 2020

Two days ago, my brother in law, Carl, had a biking accident. He passed out while biking and was found face down in the grass. He was in a neighborhood and people stepped in to help. They called 911, called my sister, and he was transported to the hospital. BP 90/40. He was released after several hours, a CT scan and blood work. Even the MD preferred not to keep him for observation due to the virus.

They see the regular MD today, so praying for some answers as to the etiology of the passing out.

Francie bringing my lunch as a thank you for something that I did for her. I can't even remember what.

Saturday, June 27, 2020

Took dinner up to Donna and Carl as they are still recovering from the bike accident. More follow-up testing to try and determine cause of low BP, as well as a scheduled visit to a cardiologist.

Sylvia came over in the afternoon and brought dinner. We talked a lot, laughed, worried about the world and our kids, and just generally had a good visit. She left about 10:00 p.m., so a late night for me and for Barkley, but well worth it!

Sunday, June 28, 2020

Ben and a friend, Kady, took Rascal out on the boat for the first time. Kady loves Rascal, so she was a good choice to take care of him during this initial ride. He did fine and had fun!!

Monday, June 29, 2020

I got a call from Monty, June's son. She is in ICU under a breathing tent with pneumonia and a fever. Test for COVID-19 not back yet. She is eight-seven years old and has been like a grandmother to Ben.

Tuesday, June 30, 2020

Today is Mom's birthday.

Mom's death was different than Dad's. She did not know us the last three years of her life. She lived to the age of eighty-four. I think my grief for my mom began while she was still alive. Ben and I had driven to Morganton, where Mom was in assisted living. We walked in the door and got our hugs and smiles. Another patient in the facility was standing there and I knew that he had a daughter who also lived in Mt. Pleasant. So, I said something about our new bridge connecting MP to Charleston to make conversation with John. My mom looked me straight in the eye, and said, "I have a daughter who lives in Mt. Pleasant and her name is Vickie Guerry. Do you know her?" The shock, the pain, the disbelief, the denial. My own mother did not know me. For three more years, we traveled to North Carolina to see Mom, knowing she wouldn't know us. The last time that we took her to a local restaurant to eat, she managed to pour the entire contents of peppermints into her empty pocketbook while smiling at the cashier. Thank goodness he was a kind person. Events like this helped us to laugh through the awful years of dementia, but this too was a part of grief.

I was not there for Mom's death. When we got the call to come home, Wendell and I quickly left work, packed, filled the car with gas and got on the road for the five-hour drive. We pulled into the facility to find my brother-in-law waiting outside, and he told me to run. I did not make it, and even though the words said to me were that she wouldn't have known, I knew and I felt that I let her down. All these years later, that stays with me.

It had been a difficult road losing Mom, very different from Dad. But even though it was expected, unlike Dad's which was a shock, it was no easier. Now, I had no parent. Listening to my second husband's words at Mom's service while my first husband served as a pallbearer was also bizarre. At Dad's funeral, my second husband was again the minister, and my first husband was by my side.

Mom and June had developed a special friendship. June went on church bus trips with Mom, they shared being grandmothers to Ben, they laughed together and enjoyed each other's company. As I hold vigil here in our home alone, thinking of June, thinking of Monty alone in her hospital room, it feels strange that it is my mom's birthday. But somehow, that is ok.

June is gone. Have talked with Monty several times. Ben left work and came here so we could be together.

Wednesday, July 1, 2020

Another family death. I am relieved that June did not have the virus, as I know Monty would have felt guilt about that since he was with her every day. He did her grocery shopping, picked up her mail and meds, took care of her apartment. A very good son to a very good mom. He told me yesterday that his mom was the one person he had to go to, to talk with, who was always there. He said that she never told him what to do, but that she always listened and tried to steer him in the right direction.

She was a strong woman. She lived through two divorces, one due to alcohol and one due to women. She survived the death of her youngest son and the loss of her parents. She lost her baby brother. Through it all, she was one of the sweetest, kindest people in the world.

She was a grandmother to Ben, as Wendell's parents had passed. When we were married, June and Amy were the family on Wendell's side in attendance. She was at the hospital the day Ben was born. She never missed a birthday party, a Halloween, or Easter and spent several Christmases with us. After she moved to Florida and could still drive to Charleston, she would come a couple of times per year and stay with us for a week or more. When Ben was born, my mom was his only living grandparent, so June took the role on as second grandmother. And she was wonderful at it. We spent our first Thanksgiving without Wendell at her apartment in Florida.

I'm going to miss her so, and I don't know what Monty is going to do. June loved me and accepted me, something that some others in his family never did. She told me that I was the best thing to ever happen to Wendell and I am eternally grateful to her for her love, companionship and friendship.

Thursday, July 2, 2020

Today was one of those days. I found myself overwhelmed with memories, eyes staying full of tears, and difficulty breathing.

A few days ago, I received another box of converted VHS tapes from IMemories. I had watched one that included a Christmas when June stayed with us. But today, I watched a tape of a church service before we were married. A deaf appreciation service. Wendell and I had worked together as a part of a committee to make the day happen. We had a large deaf population in our church and we wanted to honor them. This committee was when our friendship began. I was chairman of the committee, and he was pastor of the church. In the tape, Ben can not only see his parents ten years before he was born but can see us young! What overwhelmed me was Wendell's voice. The difference in his young voice, the speed at which he spoke and the ability to project. In his last years, every breath was a struggle, every word an effort. There was also an amazing difference in his walking, going down stairs and his stride. I am grateful that Ben can see and hear his dad as a young (forty-year-old) man.

What an amazing gift to have this tape. I may watch it every day, if I can get over the shakes.

I'm not doing well, am I?

Friday, July 3, 2020

I haven't mentioned sleeping too much. After Tom died and I was not sleeping, my doctor prescribed a light sleeping pill that is not addictive. I take half of a pill nightly, and most nights that does the trick.

Not last night. Went to sleep around 10:00 p.m. Woke up at 2:00, took the other half at 3:30, still awake at 4:30. Got up before 6:00. That tape was so much on my mind. Ben and I had watched the tape together last night. But at 2:00 a.m., it all came flooding back. The friendship that developed, that grew into love, the fun that we had, the silliness, the time. Oh, to have found each other earlier, but the sensible part of me says that would never have worked. For one thing, I am twelve years younger. So, age-wise, if he was thirty, I was eighteen. Now that's weird. Another thing is that he would not have had the girls. So, I guess one can't argue with the way things happened.

But, I reason, we could have had longer at the back end. If he had not been so ill, if if if. I see eighty-year-olds still enjoying life, but that was not to be for us. The tapes are good, helpful, comforting and also difficult, sad and upsetting.

What a mess.

Saturday, July 4, 2020

I Just finished watching *Hamilton*, the musical. What a production! What talent! One thing that really touched me was Eliza Hamilton. She lost Alexander when he was young, and she continued to write her own legacy, to help others—including starting the first orphanage in NYC. I didn't lose my husband at a young age, and I am too old to write my legacy, however, maybe it gave me some encouragement to try and do some things for others and not just sit down and die.

Sunday, July 5, 2020

Productive Sunday. Got a lot done in the study, vacuumed, omelets for dinner. Ben off today.

Monday, July 6, 2020

I had a really good hour or so with Donna this afternoon. She came by to bring us some green beans, and we sat and watched a DVD home video from thirty years ago. Looking at Mom with her grandchildren, hearing Wendell's voice as he stood behind the camera, was all good. We also talked a lot about past "situations" in our lives and how they had affected so many events. It was good to have that time.

Ben got a text as we were eating dinner that two of the managers from his business had tested positive for COVID-19. He has not seen them for three weeks but is going to be tested tomorrow anyway. It looms ever closer.

Tuesday, July 7, 2020

I feel the need to write this to Ben. No matter what this test result shows, I want to be able to take care of you. My one concern that I have about my own death is leaving you until you are settled with a person who loves you and that you equally love. You have had far too much pain in the last calendar year. I don't want to add more.

But other than you, I am ready to go. I don't know what happens when one dies, no one does. I only know that a large part of every waking minute, I am so grieving for your dad, for our life, for his arms. If there is even a chance of our being together again, I want that.

So, don't grieve for me. Miss me and know that you made my life worth living in so many ways. A child has never been more loved by both parents.

One of Tom's sermons included these words:

> The hymn "God of Grace and God of Glory" contains these words:
>
> "*Fears and doubts too long have bound us.*"
>
> With that on our minds, we are tempted to say the sooner we're out of here the better. But the hymn continues with a prayer:
>
> "*Grant us wisdom, grant us courage, For the living of these days.*"

Thursday, July 9, 2020

Terri and Larry's forty-third wedding anniversary!!

I am staying busy painting shelves in the study. I think it is going to be a much brighter room.

I just took a call from Mitch. He had his floors done in his house, plank flooring and carpet in two bedrooms. He talked about how it brightened up his house and how he needed the light. He also told me that he had read that as we age, we want more light. I found this interesting, as during the last six months to a year of Tom's life, he was always asking me to turn on more lights. And since his death, I have made conscious decisions to lighten up the house with paint and new rugs and chairs. It's not only clean and new, it is light and bright.

Friday, July 10, 2020

I may or may not have mentioned this, but butterflies and wildflowers were symbols of our love very early on. They were "our thing."

Yesterday afternoon, magic happened. I was sitting on the porch talking with Donna about Carl's upcoming heart cath., and as I gazed over towards the wildflower garden (which is actually a mess of weeds with a brick wall so high that I can't see any flowers), two beautiful orange butterflies flew all around the garden. I was on the phone for forty-five minutes and they stayed the entire time. I told Donna that Wendell was thinking about them, and this was how he let us know. I like to think that he was also telling me that he loved me.

Sometimes, you have to grab hold of these coincidences.

Saturday, July 11, 2020

Ben is off today and we made a lot of progress in the study. White coat of paint almost done. It's a mess but it is getting there.

Sunday, July 12, 2020

More painting. Started on the grey walls today. As Ben is off again, we are taking advantage of the time to work. He had his boat day with the guys on Friday. Now he will be working ten days in a row.

Monday, July 13, 2020

I am still trying to deal with this IRS stimulus check. Everything seems difficult these days.

Carl and Donna at MUSC for his heart cath.

I got a text from Donna and he has NO Blockages! Thankful for good news!

Tuesday, July 14, 2020

So, what am I doing to help others during these pandemic days?

I follow the guidelines by mearing a mask and by staying home all that I can.

I wash hands frequently.

I socially distance when meeting neighbors while walking.

I donate money to causes that are working to help this disaster.

I reach out by email, phone and handwritten notes.

I donate items that may benefit organizations.

I try to encourage.

Not too much is it?

Wednesday, July 15, 2020

Skeeter and his family were scheduled to bring lunch and have a long visit tomorrow. Skeeter was one of Tom's students who has maintained contact with me. They are at Pawley's Island for the week. Back-and-forth texts determined that it is not the safe thing to do. They have two kids and Charleston is a hotbed for the coronavirus. Maybe we can see each other in the fall.

Thursday, July 16, 2020

I am beginning to question why I am writing this. Is it doing me any good? Is anything? Do I honestly think that my words and my ramblings will ever help another person walk this path? It's just too much. The virus, the hatred, the polarization, the racism, the dishonesty, the climate, the loneliness, the need to have another chance at life, the random thoughts of how I messed up. I hate this. I hate feeling like this. I don't want to upset anyone, to take anyone's time. We are all stressed. We are all worried. So how do I keep going? I stay busy enough. Painted in the study this a.m. for several hours. Cleaned the house yesterday. I read. I sleep. I eat. I want Wendell.

Friday, July 17, 2020

Yesterday was a bummer of a day, so perhaps today will be better. Something that is a sign, a bit of good news, a call from a friend.

So, got the good news!

Samp's prostate cancer has not spread and they are conducting radiation treatments. He feels good and is only working part-time. Hopefully, he and Tina can see the grandkids, travel when it is safe and enjoy some life together. That's what I encouraged him to do. What I would have given for a few more years with Wendell.

Saturday, July 18, 2020

Enjoyed a long conversation with Linda this a.m. She has a huge decision to make regarding her mom and her retirement home. Should they bring her to live with them? Is she better off to stay there? This virus has changed so many lives and made so very many decisions difficult. No one knows what is right or wrong. No one knows what to do. There are no answers. We have to listen to the scientists and experts and do what we can as individuals to make this go away. I will never understand those who refuse to wear masks, stay out of large gatherings, practice social distancing. Our economy would be in better shape if people complied. More importantly, so many lives could have been saved.

Sunday, July 19, 2020

Another Sunday, and another Sunday listening to the sermon online. I don't know if anyone could have imagined or predicted anything like this virus. So much has changed, in a relatively quick period of time. Most of the people that I know are trying to follow the guidelines and stay safe, as well as keep others safe. Most people are also trying to stay sane, to live, to reach out to others. Many people that I know are fighting their own battles of loneliness, fear and even anger.

What do we do? What choices do we have? I continue to believe in a higher being who is there for us, who we can pray to, who we can trust. I believe that better days are coming for our world. I pray that lessons will be learned from this experience, and that we can practice care and love, helping and listening.

Monday, July 20, 2020

Had another butterfly sighting yesterday. It may be totally silly, but I feel that it is ok to get happiness where one can.

I'm also experiencing dreams of Wendell, almost nightly. Not bad dreams, but we are just going about our daily lives. Interesting.

Watched *Sleepless in Seattle* last night and when Tom Hanks' dead wife appears to him, I cried. What an emotional wreck I am.

Tuesday, July 21, 2020

Had a dental appointment today. As I told my dental hygienist, Liz, "It is sad when you are excited to go to the dentist!" My first appointment since March! Guess I better call and schedule some other past-due appointments.

They did a wonderful job of making you feel safe with all the protocols they had in place.

What a world!

Wednesday, July 22, 2020

Woke up this morning with Shandy on my mind. She was a blond cocker spaniel that Wendell gave to me the first Christmas that we were married. She was a different kind of dog. She knew about twenty-five signs in ASL and with no voice command would follow them. She fell eighteen feet (Wendell measured) out of a live oak tree and dislocated her hip. He took her to Columbia for surgery. She would ride on a flat tray he had put on the back of his bike and stay up there. We would ride on Meeting and King Streets downtown on Sunday afternoons when there was no traffic and everything was closed. (Those were the days.) One day, Shandy was outside in the yard while Wendell was remodeling our James Island house. He threw a piece of plywood out of the upstairs window and it caught her in the head. Knocked her out. He rushed her to the vet and when she woke up she was fine! Later she got Parvo and lost 2/3 of her body weight. She spent weeks at the vet's office with an IV in her paw. (Not her signing paw, ☺.) I would leave work and go to the vet's office, crawl in the cage and sit with her for hours. She could not lift her head, but she would let me put it on my lap, and I sang and talked to her while I rubbed her. On Labor Day, the vet called and asked us to come and to bring some kind of food she really liked. We took cheese and drove there, and she was standing in the back yard. We barely knew her she was so very thin. But she recovered. She died of cancer in 1996 at ten years old. She was some dog. Wish I could have "willed" Wendell back to health. He always gave me credit for Shandy living through that Parvo.

Exercise day. Walked Barkley, vacuumed the house, did some mowing, weed eating and pulling of weeds. May read the rest of the day.

Thursday, July 23, 2020

I have started reading *A Spiritual Journey* by Thomas Merton. We visited the monastery where he lived in Kentucky, the Abbey of Gethsemani, during one of our visits to see Ben while he was in seminary.

This copy was given to Wendell by a grateful student in 1991.

Friday, July 24, 2020

Ben took me out on the boat again this morning. Beautiful ride for a couple of hours. Then we saw lightning in the distance and headed in. I later learned that he had seen on the boat's GPS/weather that there were water spouts! Wow. Guess it was a good idea not to tell me that!

Saturday, July 25, 2020

Death toll from the virus continues to mount, as well as number of confirmed cases. Still no mask mandate from the governor. NYC in much better shape than Charleston, as they have put restrictions in place and lowered their numbers. If people could just do the simple things, to keep all well and safe. I read in the newspaper this a.m. that our hospitals are maxed out.

People who need to be admitted are being told to try other hospitals, some out of state! Scary times.

Sunday, July 26, 2020

I began my morning with a random selection of one of Tom's sermons. This one from 2016.

This was a portion of the sermon:

> "I suspect that as Jesus moves among us today he must weep as he did that day in Jerusalem. For surely, he weeps over the world
>
> - Where terror threatens, and people kill each other out of fear
>
> - Where missiles fly and bombs fall on the innocent as well as the guilty
>
> - Where every day thousands die of hunger
>
> - Where those who have more than we need turn deaf ears to the cries of the poor
>
> - Where in the words of Isaiah, truth stumbles in the marketplace and justice stands afar off
>
> - Where Christians set themselves against one another

- Where anger and bitterness find a home

- Where forgiveness goes lacking and reconciliation is rare

- Where judgment is made harsh and grace is made cheap.

Surely he weeps even yet."

Monday, July 27, 2020

Donna called today and Alex has tested positive for the virus. It is so prevalent, I knew before long we would know someone who had it. Annie and the kids are fine so far. Alex is asymptomatic, and he is working from home. It is so scary, every day. Donna and Carl are taking extra precautions of not being around anyone, as they have been with Annie and the kids within the past two weeks.

Guess we wait and see where this takes us. Nothing we can do at this point except pray.

Tuesday, July 28, 2020

It continues to amaze me what thoughts I wake up with. One year ago, Wendell was still in the hospital. He had gone in June 24th after getting his MD to agree to let him wait until after Betsy and JD's wedding and his last sermon on the 23rd of June. He was in the hospital for over six weeks. His pulmonologist wanted to try one more round of intensive medications intravenously. So, June 23 was the last time that he ever slept in our bed. He came home in early August to a hospital bed downstairs, as he did not have the strength to climb stairs.

I question that entire process. Did the infusions buy him some time? If not, it took time away from our being together. We will never know, and we made decisions based on what we believed was best. I have to accept that, as I have to accept a lot of things right now.

Wednesday, July 29, 2020

I received a surprise email from an old friend of Wendell's. They were high school buddies, sang together in quartets, and roomed together their freshman year at Clemson. His wife died of cancer four years ago, and he told me that he is still in pain. He understands! He came to Charleston in early October last year and visited with Wendell one morning while I worked. I think they both enjoyed the time to talk and to remember. That was the last time that Donnye and Wendell saw each other. So very glad that he made that trip.

It was good to hear from him, and good to hear from someone who has been there, is still there and understands.

Thursday, July 30, 2020

Ben was off work today and spent his day working in the study. Painting is finished and new fan and lights installed. Progress.

I washed windows and reflected on various things, including what I want to do with the remaining years of my life.

I also watched John Lewis's funeral service—maybe that's why I did so much reflecting. An amazing man who truly gave his life for his community and his nation.

Friday, July 31, 2020

July is gone. I wish the heat was gone.

Saturday, August 1, 2020

Facebook memories reminded me that Wendell had one more night in the hospital. A year ago, today, Ben, Amy and I, along with Woody and Camille, worked to turn a sunroom into a hospital room. Amy took the organ, Ben and Woody moved the piano to the other end of the room, wicker furniture was removed, plants removed or relocated, tables and lamps relocated. We set up a pretty nice area, with a room full of windows. He could see his bird feeder, the back yard and deck and all the critters that ran around out there. His oxygen tanks were set up, a bedside table with a lamp, the hospital bed with new sheets and blanket and his pillows. We did all that we could to make him comfortable.

Sunday, August 2, 2020

Wendell got home one year ago today. It was so great to have him at home, to be able to fix food that we thought he might eat, to talk. He was weak, but so happy to be at home. Barkley was happy too! She slept downstairs beside his bed! I tried to sleep on the couch, then the recliner. Not much sleep for me though.

Monday, August 3, 2020

Our first storm of the season brought much-needed rain and that's about all.

I actually got a haircut today, the first since March 19! It feels good.

Tuesday, August 4, 2020

Ben had his first boating accident a few days ago. Cut his hand pretty deeply on a propeller. He seems ok, and it appears to be healing without infection. He saw a MD the next a.m. after it happened and they said he had cleaned it well. They also said that they could not do stitches four to six hours after the incident. We never knew that!

Wednesday, August 5, 2020

The loneliness is just overwhelming. This virus and social distancing has certainly affected us all. Add to that the loss of my best friend, my partner, my lover, my strength, and some days I just don't want to go on. I need desperately to get to the mountains, but I would be alone there too. I'm forever alone.

This has happened to countless others. Each situation is different and each individual that experiences death and grief handle it differently. I think I'm doing ok. I go through the motions. I respond "fine" when people say, "How are you?" But I am dying inside. I cannot keep burdening others with my pain, my grief, my sadness. It is mine. It cannot be shared. It cannot be talked out. It cannot be prayed out.

I wonder sometimes what Wendell would have done if I had gone first.

Thursday, August 6, 2020

Some days are just better or easier than others. Yesterday was a bad one.

Friday, August 7, 2020

The days all seem the same. This virus is so containing. The hatred in the country seems more intense and constantly spreading, along with COVID. This election year appears to be headed for the all-time high list of nastiness, lies, trolling. So many of the ways that we held ourselves together, time with family and friends, worshipping together, traveling, exploring new ideas, helping others, working together, all have vanished.

For others like me, who are already struggling with the loneliness and the void, all the negatives are increased significantly.

Saturday, August 8, 2020

Thirty-four years ago, today, we closed on our James Island house, attended the rehearsal for our wedding, and attended the rehearsal dinner at Debbie and Mike Kollar's house. A day filled with excitement and expectation. A day filled with family, close friends, laughter and a lot of love.

I was contacted by three people unexpectedly today. One, an old friend from a former church. She and her husband shared our anniversary date and she remembered and reached out to let me know that she was thinking of me. Another was a current church friend who did not know the date. Said I came into her mind and she felt something "strange" as she put it. I explained what I was going through. Amy texted tonight and said, "Are you ok?" Not sure if she remembered the date, or if she felt something too. All of the contacts helped.

Sylvia came and we had an appetizer dinner. Good to have a few hours with her.

Sunday, August 9, 2020

Today would have been our thirty-fourth wedding anniversary. Ben and I drove down to the church and visited his grave. We sat in the church and talked about thirty-four years ago when I walked down that aisle to see Wendell waiting for me. A glorious, fun, love-filled day. I watched our wedding video. I responded to texts from my sisters and a couple of friends who remembered. I posted nothing on FB. It is too private a day to share.

It is a strange feeling to have your anniversary without your partner. The day will remain special to me, but it will never be the same. Anniversaries are meant to be shared, to talk about the past, to make your partner watch the wedding video, to drink champagne and toast to many more years together. I did read the anniversary cards that I have and read his words to me. Sometimes I do believe that he loved me!

Monday, August 10, 2020

Yard work, dogs, reading, nap. That basically describes this day.

Tuesday, August 11, 2020

Finally, good news about the virus. Percentage of cases dropped to 12 percent from a high of 21 percent. Deaths decreasing. If only we can stay smart and maintain the safety precautions. School starting back at MSA today, totally online.

Heading to design center with Ben this a.m. to pick out carpet for the study!

Wednesday, August 12, 2020

I spoke too soon. Our percentage is back up to 20 percent. Hopefully we will see a downward trend, but with school restarting and talk of fall sports, I just don't know.

Andrea came over for happy hour. We watched the Biden/Harris introduction together. Hoping and praying for some big changes in our country.

Thursday, August 13, 2020

We painted the shelves and got them up in the study.

Elise and Betsy came by for a visit.

Today is the birthday of the deceased wife of a neighbor. This is her second birthday that he has been without her. I feel for him, but other than a text to let him know that I am thinking of him and his daughters, nothing to do.

Friday, August 14, 2020

Donna and Carl invited me to dinner. Nice to have a few hours to chat and eat good food.

Saturday, August 15, 2020

Plans are underway to destroy the effectiveness of the US Post Office. I would never in my wildest dreams imagined the awful events occurring in my country today. In order to win an election, to deflect votes, sorting machines are being removed from post offices to slow the process. No overtime is permitted and positions are being cut.

Locally, a black community, formed generations ago, land bought by freed slaves, is being parted once again. A five-lane highway has been approved to go through their land, replacing their homes, taking their yards. The five lanes were approved to go a different route, in order to preserve wetlands and this community, but the rich, white homeowners didn't want it going through their land and for their children to be near a five-lane highway. But it's ok for it to happen to the Philips community?

I fear my grief extends beyond the loss of my husband. It engulfs the loss of my country.

Sunday, August 16, 2020

Cleaned windows inside and out yesterday so am terribly sore today. Had an easy day of reading, taking care of the dogs, devotional, and chicken and dumplings in the crock pot for Ben and me.

Monday, August 17, 2020

I am surrounded by books. This is not a new revelation of course, but I suddenly this morning became aware of this being yet another gift from my husband. As I continue to downsize, I am at a place where I can slowly go through books on shelves all over this home. Several times, including this morning, I think, oh I would like to read that book.

A gift indeed.

Tuesday, August 18, 2020

I have repeatedly commented that grief is personal, and that it truly cannot be shared. I continue to be grateful and to appreciate those who still know that my journey is not finished, that I still have constant pain and that the loneliness is only beginning. But I struggle to find the words to share what this experience has done to me. Countless others have lost someone they loved with all of their hearts. The ones of us lucky enough to have known this deep love face this deep grief, but also, we deny this in our own ways. The facing of this loss is fluid. There are minutes where we function, followed by minutes where we can't. There are minutes where we are moving and living, followed by minutes where we don't.

A journey I would not wish on anyone. And yet, if this journey was not crushing me, I would never have known his love.

Wednesday, August 19, 2020

COVID draws ever nearer. Yesterday evening Ben came in from work and reported that his assistant manager had been tested for COVID-19. He had a bad throat, was tested for strep and that was negative. He was tested for COVID and sent home for three days or until results get back. If he is positive, then Ben and coworkers, as well as their families will have to be tested. Cancelled my trip to Louise's house this morning to get okra.

Thursday, August 20, 2020

So many things affect me in ways that are new and different from how I might have viewed them prior to Tom's death. I have talked about how I respond to songs. I recall shopping in Harris Teeter one day a few weeks before he died. The song "Through the Years" by Kenny Rogers came over the intercom. I burst into tears and I stood facing the shelves until I could get myself under control. I cannot recall ever having that experience before. When I got home, I told Tom, "I just lost it in Harris Teeter".

Reading has been a love of mine since I first learned to read. Growing up, our house was beside the town library and I couldn't believe how lucky a girl I was. There have been very few books that reduced me to tears, although I do recall one. Ben and I read every night and we read "Where the Red Fern Grows", and both of us cried at the end. I still love that book.

So, I was reading "The Giver of Stars" by JoJo Moyes. It is a wonderful book, that fills you with all kind of emotions. In one particular scene Kathleen, who has just lost her husband, is talking with Alice. She talks about how she misses him so much, misses his touch, misses his hair, misses the way he said her name. She sobs for a long time, and then apologizes to Alice for breaking down. Alice's response was filled with not only kindness, but understanding and compassion, while giving Kathleen a life line. She said "It's wonderful that you got to love somebody that much."

Those words have stayed with me, and created something positive for me to ponder. I was lucky enough to love somebody that much, and I have a growing awareness of how many people never know that kind of love.

I am in awe sometimes to realize all the different turns our individual lives took, in order for us to end up together. We were blessed beyond measure.

Friday, August 21, 2020

Ben's coworker does not have COVID! YEAH!

We had planned to take a boat ride today but cancelled due to Ben's car in shop. So, we cleaned out the garage. A hot, sweaty, but much overdue task!

Saturday, August 22, 2020

Sometimes when I sit down to write these daily thoughts and feelings, I do believe that I have become a whiner. Poor me. Look at my life. Look at what I lost. But, at least no one is reading them except me. It is a good way to get some of my emotions out.

I don't want to be like this for the rest of my life.

Drove to Johns Island and had a healing visit with Louise, sitting on her porch looking at the water. Got my okra and came home.

Sunday, August 23, 2020

Happy Birthday to my brother-in-law, Larry! We had planned to all be together to celebrate, but this dang virus.

Monday, August 24, 2020

Rainy, overcast day. Gonna make some okra soup.

Ben's friend Drew getting out of hospital today after gallstone surgery. Maybe he would eat some soup.

Tuesday, August 25, 2020

As I work through this process, I have become aware that some thoughts and feelings are too private, even for the individual writings. Some memories are all mine and not meant to share or to write down. Some thoughts, both good and bad, take me to a deep secret place. A place of reflection, of agony, of prayer, of joy. Wisdom has come slowly to me in life. I have lived, and loved, and laughed. But there are oh so many words that I would have spoken if I had been permitted to do so. So many persons that I might have helped, if I had the courage to work harder and longer, to speak out more freely, to love harder and deeper, to dream dreams that could have come true. With wisdom comes regret, sadness, anger. With wisdom comes thankfulness, happiness, love.

Wednesday, August 26, 2020

Ben was tested for COVID yesterday. They told him it might be seven to ten days before he gets a response. In the meantime, he is working from home. He feels good. His coworker is still feeling pretty bad.

He came over mid-morning and worked from here. Also did some chores, cleaned his boat, helped me take up old carpet in the office. So good to have him around.

I also learned from Samp that an old friend is dying. He has had several strokes. I have not seen him for years, but my thoughts are with his family and his close friends, like Samp.

They were like brothers. Hospice has been called in and Shana is his social worker. Small world. Glad that she is there to care for this family.

It's been quite a year. Wendell, June, COVID, divorce, friends dying, politics.

Thursday, August 27, 2020

Hurricane Laura, a category 4, slammed Louisiana early this morning. Storm surge is very high. This is a bad one. Prayers for all of those in harm's way.

Friday, August 28, 2020

Mowed back yard this morning. Ben has a friend, Grant, coming in for the weekend, so things will be quiet around here. He needs this time with his buddy. Hopefully the weather will hold so they can boat.

Ben's COVID test is negative!!!!!!!!! So grateful!

Saturday, August 29, 2020

Watched my first Zoom wedding today. One of Tom's cousins' daughter was getting married and after several postponements due to COVID, they decided to make it a Zoom wedding. It was lovely and their happiness and love came through. I'm not sure that I did it correctly, as my picture never showed up on the screen, but that's fine. My name did so they knew I was there. I wanted to represent Tom.

Sunday, August 30, 2020

Quiet Sunday. I was trying to recover from vacuuming and mowing in the same day. Good day to read and nap.

Monday, August 31, 2020

Ben took the day off from work and we made marinara sauce to can. Francie and Tony brought me a box of mountain tomatoes.

My pressure canner broke earlier this summer and stupid me didn't look for a new one. Not one to be found now, even online. I guess more folks are canning with this virus keeping them in, plus parts are difficult to find, and especially with metal products. So, have to borrow Donna's.

Tuesday, September 1, 2020

Is it really September? Got the marinara sauce canned. Drove up to Donna and Carl's early this a.m. to borrow canner so I could get busy. We ended up with seven quarts and a bag to freeze. I have never done this before. I have canned many things but never made homemade marinara sauce. This was a Ben idea and it tasted good!

Wednesday, September 2, 2020

I love seeing the butterflies! Butterflies and wildflowers were important signs of our love. These little sightings and unexpected events are making me smile now instead of tear up. Today in the grocery store I saw the new Farmer's Almanac for sale. Every year I had to put one in Tom's stocking. Another smile. I do like being reminded of him and it makes me feel that he is always around.

Thursday, September 3, 2020

Reading the newest Louise Penny novel. Reading is such a positive support for me. I can lose myself in a book and it takes away the pain for a bit.

Friday, September 4, 2020

Racism is all around us. It lunges into our everyday lives, our newspapers, our pimento cheese. It is fed by leaders who strive to create unrest, to instill fear, to plot neighbor against neighbor.

I found these words of Tom's today.

"As we sang just moments ago:

I sing the goodness of the Lord

That filled the earth with food;

He formed the creatures with his word.

And then pronounced them good."

A familiar anecdote recalls the time a lady asked Benjamin Franklin if we have a republic or a monarchy. His answer was: "A republic, if you can keep it."

One might ask a similar question of the Bible. When God created the heavens and the earth, what do we have, paradise or perdition? The answer would seem obvious enough, "Paradise, if you can keep it."

And yet, as we know all too well, the dark clouds of racism and the terrible blight of hatred is with us to obscure the goodness of creation. Every time we hear voices of hatred we grieve. Every time we hear of another act of violence we are tempted to despair. What we have seen in our city and others, is rightly viewed as an assault on persons. But every act of racism is to shake one's fist in the face of God and to challenge the goodness of his creation. WTG 11/4/2018

Saturday, September 5, 2020

The new carpet in the study was installed yesterday. I love it. Another big step towards getting the office completed.

Ben and I have reservations for Sullivan's tonight. It will be the first time that I have been in a restaurant since March or maybe before that. I hope we will be safe.

Sullivan's is a family-owned restaurant on Sullivan's Island. The food is consistently good and the prices are not as bad as many. Tom and I enjoyed many a Sunday lunch there after church, and we took out-of-town friends there often. So sad it is closing but lots of places are. They will be missed.

Sunday, September 6, 2020

Another Sunday is gone. Tomorrow is Labor Day and I am concerned about the COVID numbers rising after a weekend of celebrating.

Phil preached a really good sermon today on Fear.

Monday, September 7, 2020

Donna and Carl's fortieth wedding anniversary. They were invited to go on an early-morning boat ride with me and Ben, but Donna is under the weather.

We had a lovely two-hour trip through Shem Creek and over to Charlestowne Landing.

Labor Day 2020

Tuesday, September 8, 2020

COVID percentage down to 11.2. I would so love to see it continue to decrease, but it all depends on how things turn out with school opening and with Labor Day weekend.

Wednesday, September 9, 2020

Linda coming next week for a couple of days!! I am so excited!

Thursday, September 10, 2020

Watched part of the first NFL game of the season. Everything is so very different. Fans, noise, no bands, no cheerleaders. A new world we are experiencing.

Friday, September 11, 2020

Nineteen years ago today, I was in my office at Berkeley County Schools. My secretary told me that my sister was on the phone, which was unusual for her to call me at work. She immediately said, "Kate is fine." I said, "Ok," thinking, what is she talking about? (Kate is an airline stewardess). Before she could explain, my secretary entered my office to tell me about the attacks on the Twin Trade Towers in NYC. Quickly news spread. I left work, an hour from home. Ben was in middle school. Tom was at the university teaching classes. We were all across bridges from each other. Charleston being a port city, having a navy base here, a coast guard station, and the Naval Weapons Station, we were all concerned. All that we wanted was to get the three of us home safely, and to ride this out together.

9/11 is one of those days that we always remember. Where we were, who we were with, what we were doing. We all have our stories, just like Hurricane Hugo, JFK's shooting, and other major events in our world.

Woody ended today's devotional with these words:

> "No matter what happens in life, we can always turn to God for comfort. Sometimes we forget that fact and we try to get through difficult times and tough situations alone. We know there is strength in numbers. We need to remember that God loves us, God is with us, and God will walk with us."

Saturday, September 12, 2020

It's a football Saturday! The first of 2020. What a strange, different time we are living.

Sunday, September 13, 2020

It's a Sunday and I mowed the back yard this a.m. in preparation for Linda's visit. I would never have done that growing up (we couldn't go to the movies on Sundays) or when Wendell was alive. Sundays were a church day, a day of family and rest. Well, I can listen to the service anytime today, and I have to spread out the work, so that is my justification. Wendell is probably frowning at me now.

I find it interesting that he is in my thoughts all of the time. Every decision I make, every conversation that I have, every meal that I eat. I don't mind. I hope this is always the way it continues until I die. It gives me a sense of him.

Monday, September 14, 2020

One of those days when everything I planned to do went south. There are days like that.

Ben did trade his BMW, which was giving him all kinds of trouble, for a red pick-up truck. Will do better pulling the boat. I was concerned about how the orange Clemson stickers would work on a red truck, but of course he has that figured out.

He left the dealership after getting the truck and was on the way to work when he realized that he had left something. It was the orange tiger paw decal that his dad had on his red truck.

When the truck was sold, Ben put it on his BMW. He turned around and went back, as he was not leaving his dad's tiger paw.

Tuesday, September 15, 2020

Linda's not coming. Looks like a couple of hurricanes might visit us with heavy rain and flooding. As she will be driving the coastal roads from Wilmington, we both agreed it was not the best idea. Very disappointed, but better to be safe than sorry. I don't want to lose her. She says perhaps in October she will try and visit.

Wednesday, September 16, 2020

This reflection about Wendell was shared by Fred Shuszler, minister, author and friend.

In our brief time working together at First Baptist Church of Morganton, I have many memories of interesting, inspiring experiences we shared and lots of humorous experiences we enjoyed (or endured) that still bring a smile or chuckle. Here is one quick one: As an unexperienced minister of youth, I'll admit I wasn't always in full control over my young, unruly charges. Once, on a Wednesday evening "Church Family Night," a group of wild young'uns and I were crowded into the church office working on a learning project. (I think we were in the office to use some of the equipment there like the copier or the cutting board.) In the office, hidden behind a painting, was the buzzer button we used on Sunday mornings to push/ring when Sunday School was supposed to conclude. As far as I know, the teens had no idea it was there, but accidentally one of them bumped into the painting (probably because they were bouncing on the sofa!) and once that happened they couldn't keep from pushing the buzzer whenever my back was turned. I remember being somewhat distracted, telling them to stop pushing the button, but not really minding, since the adults were way over in the fellowship hall and we were in the main building. It was irritating, but what was the harm?

Then I remember the office door opening and a big shadow being cast into the office. The kids immediately got silent and scrambled to look busy—probably flipping pages in their Bibles with their best intensive "studying" faces on. The big shadow was Wendell. He surveyed the kids with a stern look but turned to me with a cool, grim, semi-smile, and after a pregnant pause in his best "Lurch" (the butler character from the Addams Family television show) accent said, "You rang?" It turns out he was trying to lead a Bible study in the fellowship hall and that alarm kept going off (who knew it could be heard all the way over there?!). I was mortified and tried to explain but didn't really need to. Wendell let the humor of the ridiculous situation overcome the uncomfortable irritation of the situation. What would've surely gotten me into a world of trouble in any other church, with any other senior minister, became a grace-filled demonstration of Wendell's tolerant nature. Thanks for letting me off the hook, Wendell!

Thursday, September 17, 2020

Lots of progress made on my study desk by Ben and Woody! It is built, now to be painted and the top stained. Exciting! Thank you, guys!

Friday, September 18, 2020

Ben and Emily managed to have a lengthy, cordial conversation last night by text and by FaceTime. He said it was painful, but also healing. She is in a committed relationship and is planning her future. I think every ounce of closure helps, and there is a difference in the hurt if it excludes the anger and meanness, and insults. I feel good about this because he told me that it was good. I, as any parent, just want his happiness.

Ruth Bader Ginsburg died today. A remarkable, strong, brilliant woman who gave everything for this country. May her work not be in vain.

Saturday, September 19, 2020

We are enjoying some crisp, fall air. Gosh, it would be great if this lasted.

Sunday, September 20, 2020

Today is Tom's birthday. One year ago today, I asked him what he wanted and felt like doing. He wanted to drive by the church one more time and to drive up to North Charleston and see the new train station. So, Ben and I took him. It was no small task to get him in the car, and it was the last time he was in his Jetta. We had to get him into the wheelchair, go to the door leading into the garage, move him into a chair, move the wheelchair into the garage, get him down the stairs with a cane, the railing and one of us behind and one of us in front of him. Into the wheelchair, and then into the car. Then we added the portable oxygen tank, and anything else that he wanted or needed. We placed the wheelchair in the back of the car and we were off.

Once we drove to the church and train station, he wanted to drive around his old haunts in North Charleston. "This is where my piano teacher lived, this is the tree that I planted, I didn't know they tore down the football stadium," etc. This was encouraging as he kept directing Ben where he wanted to go. It was a successful outing and he had fun! He wanted to go home for lunch, though. He had done enough.

Ben is working in Summerville today. So, Amy and her family met us at his model home and we ate lunch together and visited a couple of hours. It was her suggestion for us to get together for her dad's birthday and I am so grateful to her for suggesting it.

Brenda called late afternoon to check on me. People truly have no idea what these gestures mean.

Another "first" checked off.

Monday, September 21, 2020

I feel emotionally and physically drained today. Yesterday must have been more stressful than I let on. Today I am having difficulty getting into any tasks. I did walk Barkley and the air is amazing. It was fifty-seven degrees this morning.

I heard from Linda today. She was just wanting to hear that I was ok.

Tuesday, September 22, 2020

Sylvia's daughter's twenty-first birthday. I cannot believe Rachel is twenty-one!

I continue to be amazed how life just keeps on around me. Ben had a date last night. I sold a book. Going out to cut ivy off of trees. Life.

Wednesday, September 23, 2020

Donna and Carl stopped by to pick up some bags of items that I have been saving for the Children's Museum downtown. Things like empty paper towel rolls, toilet paper rolls, lids, etc. Donna and Carl pack these things up and deliver them to the museum. The museum has put a hold on donations, as they have not been able to use what they have due to a decreased attendance (COVID) and having filled their storage area. It's a good project to know about though and can be restarted when all is well.

Thursday, September 24, 2020

Ruth Bader Ginsburg is dead. I keep repeating that. What a gift her life was to women and minorities everywhere. What a brave, exceptional human she was. What a loss to our country.

Friday, September 25, 2020

Ben worked in the study today and made some progress. Not at a place where I can help.

Saturday, September 26, 2020

Donna and Carl invited me to lunch today. After good soup and corn-bread, Donna and I sat for hours going through pictures that she had kept in a box that had been Mom's. It was fun looking at these old pictures of our parents, grandparents, great-aunts and uncles. Wendell would have loved doing that and hearing the stories that she shared. Donna had the actual letter where Daddy asked Mom to marry him… in a letter! How cool is that?

Sunday, September 27, 2020

After work, Ben and Ted put the new AC unit in the study. Getting the old one out was the issue. Tom Guerry put it in himself more than twenty years ago, and they almost gave up getting it out! When he did something, he did it right!

Monday, September 28, 2020

WOW supposed to be coming this a.m. to fix internet. It has been working intermittently for a few weeks now and after multiple phone calls and troubleshooting, I have asked for an in-house consultation. GRRR!

As I figured the tech guy asked me questions that I didn't know the answers to. Tom always dealt with this kind of stuff…where is the cable box? Anyway, nice guy and hopefully we are in good shape now.

Isn't it interesting in most partnerships, that we have our roles? He did this stuff, I did this stuff, we did this stuff. You think that you have shared everything, but in reality, we didn't. I told Ben two years ago that if something happened to me that his dad could not live alone. Now, I realize that without Ben's help, I probably could not stay in the house. Either that, or a lot of stuff would not be done.

I'm trying to not be a burden, to be independent. I thank God every day for giving us this son, and for his being the person that he is. All young people are not this caring.

Tuesday, September 29, 2020

I ate popcorn for dinner last night and watched the Cunningham/ Mace debate. Ben had a date and I don't cook for one.

Had some strange dreams about Jesus in the woods and Wendell. Maybe popcorn and politics are not a great idea before bedtime!!

Wednesday, September 30, 2020

I am loving the cooler weather. Did some yard work in the secret garden and trimmed some hedges. I give up on the yard guys ever showing up to trim these hedges…it's been months since I first called to get on their schedule.

As I watched the "presidential" debate last night, I continued to grieve for our country. Pettiness, name calling, a total disregard for basic turn-taking skills, listening skills and general human relations was missing. An embarrassment.

Thursday, October 1, 2020

It's October. As I typed in the date above, I typed in October 17. Perhaps I am projecting, but it is so hard to believe that it has been almost one year.

I submitted the following letter to the editor of the *Post and Courier* today. It probably won't be printed, but I wanted to try and say something:

> I believe in the right of every individual to vote, and to vote as they believe without coercion.
>
> I do not believe in attacking, criticizing, or belittling someone.
>
> Joe Biden is a stutterer. As a speech pathologist for more than 45 years, I have worked with multiple stutterers and their families. I know how difficult this disability is and how it never completely leaves you alone. You have to work, practice strategies, and implement them. One of the most stressful areas is to be rushed into your speech, to be interrupted, to be belittled. I am aware of his hesitations, his changing words in order to select a more easily pronounced one, his breath control. I am also aware of the inner strength and determination to deal daily with stuttering. Please don't confuse speech patterns

with dementia. When Joe Biden is given the opportunity to speak, he has words that can help to heal a divided nation.

Friday, October 2, 2020

Ben off. Productive day in the study.
President Trump has COVID.

Saturday, October 3, 2020

Nice cooler air on our walk this morning. Barkley feels frisky!
Lots and lots of butterfly sightings!

"So, this idea is you don't lose everything when someone dies. You do lose their physical presence, but their physical presence is not all of them, and it never was all of them, even when they were alive. Spirit is very strong. Emotion is very strong. Their energy is very strong. And a lot of this, particularly for people who are very powerful, really carries over after death."

The Boss
Bruce Springsteen

Monday, October 5, 2020

One year ago, today was my fiftieth high school reunion. I was not going, but Tom among others insisted that I go. I had not been to one of our reunions since our twentieth, when I was pregnant with Ben and some of my classmates were already grandmothers!

Linda and I had worked hard for months putting together a memory book. It was fun reconnecting with classmates, even just by email and snail mail. We were proud of the end result.

Linda drove from Wilmington and then we drove together to Morganton. We visited an apple orchard the morning of the reunion and almost came home when Ben called. But he called back and assured me (as much as he could) that all was fine.

The reunion was a lot of fun! I saw people that I had not seen for fifty years, and many that I had not seen for thirty! It was clouded for me by thoughts of Tom and what I had left, but we had frequent contact and I sent him tons of pictures.

Linda and I left early Sunday morning for home, and for Tom. I would never have made this trip without her, physically or mentally. I thank God for her every day.

Tuesday, October 6, 2020

Ben off work. More progress in study. The desk has one coat of polyurethane.

I worked outside and got some major weeding done.

I watched the second Cunningham/Mace debate. I, like so many others, am ready for this election to be behind us.

Wednesday, October 7, 2020

COVID numbers rising again across the country.

Why can't people, including leaders, listen to the medical experts and do the simple things such as mask?

Watched the Harris/Pence debate. More civil than the presidential debate. That fly on his head! I swatted my TV as I thought it was in my house!! Silly me!

Thursday, October 8, 2020

Busy phone day. Spent three hours talking on the phone between Linda and Brenda. Good to talk with both of them and work can just wait.

Friday, October 9, 2020

I had ordered Amy a Ruth Bader Ginsburg mask today and she texted that it had arrived. She seemed to like it!

Mac's mom, Beth, transported to MUSC today with difficulty breathing. They think it is pneumonia but COVID test has not come back. He has been so good to Ben and to me, as well as to Tom and I adore Beth.

Saturday, October 10, 2020

Beth had complications from COPD, not pneumonia. Should be going home today! So very glad!

Watched a lot of football today. The Tarheels and the Tigers both won!

Sunday, October 11, 2020

It was a quiet Sunday. Did some writing and reflecting and watched Heartland on TV. It is the beginning of the week that he died one year ago.

Monday, October 12, 2020

Sylvia texted and offered to hang out Saturday if I wanted to do so. She said she would bring deviled eggs and a pitcher of Bloody Marys. They were two of Tom's favorites. I told her I would get back to her as I don't know what is best or what is going to feel right. (I also told her that I don't like Bloody Marys!) It was a kind, generous thought. We will see what seems best.

Tuesday, October 13, 2020

I stood in line at the PO for forty-five minutes this a.m. Everyone was masked and socially distanced, but wow...Took what I hope is the last of the paperwork for Ben and Emily's divorce to Mac. COVID continues to touch every aspect of our lives and continues to change how we conduct business, run errands, and just live.

Wednesday, October 14, 2020

As we move into this week, I am hearing from friends and family. Ben and I got a sweet card from Donna and Carl yesterday, another friend sent a FB message this a.m., another friend asked if he could put flowers on Tom's grave. My year of "muddling through" is almost at a calendar end. Wish I could know inside me that I am going to be able to keep on. Oh, I know externally it looks like I am fine. I know that I am certainly functioning. But I also feel that my heart is not going to heal, that I don't have a thought or a breath that does not include him. Wasted, wasted time doing unimportant things. My telling couples, young and old, to take time for each other, to live every day like it is their last, would fall on deaf ears. We completed tasks, worked, cared for family, did church, entertained and got through the days, but if we had had the perspective that I have now, I imagine most folks would live them differently. I know that I would.

Thursday, October 15, 2020

Ben and I voted at the Coliseum today. I returned my absentee ballot and voted in person. It was a good feeling to know that my vote counted, not to worry about mail or an absentee ballot. It took us about thirty minutes. I haven't done much except make donations, but I do hope that this election will be the beginning of our country working ourselves out of this mess that we are in, and that somehow, someway, Americans can work together for our country and not in constant opposition.

Friday, October 16, 2020

It is the eve of Wendell's death. Almost one year. As I relive that last day and that last evening, I wish I had done some things differently. I should never have gone upstairs at 3:30 a.m. and left him to die alone. I am such a Martha and have always been guilty of getting things done, taking care of things, doing things myself, instead of sitting down beside him, holding his hand, and talking. I can't get that or other days back. I cannot continue to dwell on these kinds of memories while pushing aside the happy, good memories. Perhaps I will one day find a way to do that.

Somehow, I need to find the inner strength to put others first. Instead of dwelling on me and my loss, on him and our love, I have to spend my mental abilities on others. I do think of Ben and his relationships, on family and neighbors, but I think I need to do more. What will that be? What will it look like? This year has been a year of acceptance, of survival, of deep pain, of loneliness. Maybe I can find an outlet where I am needed and can make a difference. I just don't know.

Saturday, October 17, 2020

It has been one year today since I lost my love. 365 days. It looks like I have survived all of the firsts. I think that I am at a place where I can recognize good days, a hint of joy, a whiff of happiness. I see a butterfly, or a wildflower, a Farmer's Almanac for sale, a silver Jetta, an old red truck, a tiger paw, and I smile. We had a few years of dating and thirty-three years of marriage. We found each other, fell in love, and clung to that love through some very difficult times and some amazingly happy times. I am grateful for all of the memories, all of the experiences, the sharing of a son, and the gift of caring for my husband until the end. I needed this year to find me.

I am surrounded by him, his books, furniture that he made, pictures, his chair, and his presence. These bring me comfort and peace. Among other things, this year has taught me how much people mean in our lives, the contact, the words, the hugs (even virtual). By necessity, you walk a path like I am walking alone, but along that trail you become aware of people who genuinely share a tiny gesture that becomes a large buttress. May I have the empathy and the awareness to remember and to reach out to others struggling to travel their individual paths.

My year of grief has ended, but I realize that it never truly will end. He is with me in every breath that I take, and every word that I utter. I'm ok with that. It's like that old, large sweatshirt that you get to wear when the weather cools. It's comforting, and it just feels right.

The world keeps turning. Many of the subjects that I have touched on in these pages are still thrashing all of us. This pandemic, which continues to grow and affect so many lives, as well as businesses. This election, filled with unpleasantness and foulness, still looms over us and I fear may do so for a long time. But, cool air is arriving, pumpkins are growing and butterflies are abundant. As long as we can cling to some hope for the world, and for ourselves, perhaps we can hang on long enough to make our world a better place—for all living things.

To risk being redundant, you were the best part of me. For the love and passion and togetherness, the moments of sharing and chatting, of doing church together, of traveling and being at home, of decorating Christmas trees, and watching *White Christmas*, of fires and bike rides, searching for snow, and loving our dogs, for loving Amy and her family and watching your grandsons grow, for giving me a son and sharing his life and love, I am eternally grateful.

A friend recently told me that my love for you is palpable. I never thought of that, but I guess it is.

I love you Wendell Thomas Guerry, and I always will.

Forever,

Vickie

Acknowledgements

*A word of thanks is not enough to express my appreciation to Bessie
Gantt for her editing and proofing skills, her kindness,
and her support for this project.*

*Alan Garmendia was kind enough to let me use his photograph
on the cover.*

*Finally, thank you to my son, Benjamin Guerry,
in appreciation for his total support, his encouragement
and proofreading, and most of all, for his constant presence in my life.
I love you Ben.*

About the Author

Vickie Guerry grew up in the mountains, West Virginia and North Carolina. She received a BS degree from Appalachian State University, and an MS degree from the University of North Carolina. She is a retired Speech Language Pathologist, having worked for 45 years with a variety of populations at various agencies, including owning her own private practice. Having  moved to the Lowcountry of South Carolina in 1981, Vickie currently lives in Mt. Pleasant with her golden retriever, Barkley.

CPSIA information can be obtained
at www.ICGtesting.com
Printed in the USA
LVHW022358200721
693167LV00010B/809